Alberto Palazzi

Quantum Computing for Programmers and Investors

GogLiB *ebooks*

ISBN: 9788897527541

Contents

1. Introduction

An explanation for programmers and investors

Why this book is written for programmers and investors together will be fully understood after reading it. Preliminarily, let us say that regarding quantum computing there are two questions:

1) when will it be possible to build an efficient quantum computer?

2) what problems will it solve?

The books on quantum computing that have been written contain notions of a different nature: they speak in greater or less detail of the (quantum) physical principles that govern subatomic phenomena, they expose the mathematics necessary for the study of quantum physics (linear algebra), and finally they deal with quantum computing. In this book, readers will not find any notion regarding physical principles, and with regard to mathematics they will find only the applied part necessary for quantum computing, which consists of algorithms for arithmetic operations on vectors and matrices of complex numbers. Then on this basis the readers will find the description of the most famous quantum gates and quantum algorithms, with implementation in C language. The quantum computer will be described as a hardware black box that is able to transform a given input into a given output, such as it always happens in computer science texts, in which the notions concerning semiconductor electronics underlying the calculations are only hinted at and could even be completely omitted.

Therefore, this book has no answer for question 1. If ever and when shall we succeed in building an efficient quantum computer, it is such a question that requires a thorough knowledge and experience of quantum physics in order to hazard an answer.

Instead, reading this book, readers will find themselves in possession of a precise answer to the second question: if tonight the devil, as in fairy tales, built a perfectly efficient and stable quantum computer, capable of handling a matrix of qubits of considerable size, the next day for what purposes could we use it? It must be said immediately that the peculiarity of quantum hardware will be to perform in a single act, a single change of state of the machine, certain operations on matrices that today's computers based on the principle of the Turing machine must perform through the iteration of numerous cycles nested one inside the other, and therefore with considerable execution times, and for certain problems with such extended times as not to allow technically useful solutions. By performing transformations of the input corresponding to a certain (ideally very large) number of cycles of a classical computer with a single change of state, we read and hear that the quantum computer will be able to drastically cut the execution time for operations of encryption and cryptography, and for finding solutions to highly complex problems such as those of logistics, optimization, scheduling, operational research, etc.

How this could happen can be understood through the emulation of quantum algorithms using the classical computer available today, although obviously the emulation will have no practical use because the emulation of a quantum algorithm without quantum hardware will always require computing resources greater than those required to run the corresponding non-quantum algorithm. That is, suppose we need to perform a transformation of a matrix that the quantum computer will perform in a single state change of the machine. Suppose that the same transformation by an algorithm executable on a classical computer requires the repetition of, say, a thousand or a million cycles. Well, if we try to get the same result with a classical algorithm that emulates a quantum algorithm, as we shall see and as is imaginable, we shall need a number of cycles much greater than the thousand or one million of the classical algorithm, and we shall also need to allocate much more memory. We shall see below, for example, how the classic computer emulation of Shor's algorithm for finding the factors of a number is enormously less efficient than any elementary algorithm for finding prime factors.

This book is written for *programmers* because to read it you only need to have the common basics of computer science (logic gates, flowcharts, programming languages). The examples are written in C language in the simplest way and without the use of constructs that are not elementary, so that anyone who can read any programming language will understand it. The purpose of the book is to lead the reader to understand the logic of the quantum algorithms described in chapter 6, and therefore everything explained in chapters 2 to 5 is enormously simplified and reduced to the bare minimum: the deliberate choice was to give to the reader only the premises necessary to understand the logical flow and the calculations of quantum algorithms, which is supposed to be the aim of the reader, and for this reason the chapters preceding the one dedicated to quantum algorithms contain only the information that is a necessary condition for understanding.

It is important to point out that the knowledge of the purely computer science part of quantum algorithms is not subject to any limitations due to the fact that it completely disregards the physical characteristics of the hardware. The proof lies in the fact that by reading this book the readers will be able to implement and execute quantum algorithms on their PC, obtaining the results envisaged by the theory: therefore the knowledge of quantum algorithms will be so complete as to allow their application and verification. This also proves that quantum algorithms in themselves do not require quantum hardware, just as the CPU of a computer could theoretically be built by mechanical means rather than by exploiting electronic properties: but it would be too slow a machine to be useful for anything, and exactly the same happens by emulating quantum algorithms with the classical computers existing today.

Since this book allows people having the knowledge of a *programmer* to understand exactly what a quantum computer could be used for, once built, it solves at least half of the problem that investors face when evaluating whether and how much it is appropriate to risk investing in development of quantum computing. Therefore, investors (private investors, consultants, investment fund managers, managers of funds financing technology initiative, etc.), if they do not personally possess the necessary prerequisites to understand this book, could use it by summoning some IT expert they trust, and leaving to this expert the task to read it, understand it and report on the result.

Bibliography and verification

This book is a simplified presentation of the theory set out in full in two fundamental treatises, which are:

- Nielsen, Michael & Chuang, Isaac L., *Quantum Computation and Quantum Information*, Cambridge University Press, 2000 and 2010
- Yanofsky, Noson S. & Mannucci, Mirco A., *Quantum Computing for Computer Scientists*, Cambridge University Press, 2008.

Everything stated in the following in a descriptive way and as a matter of fact, without demonstrations and without quotations, can be verified and deepened through the study of these two volumes, which the reader who has assimilated this book will probably find easier than it seems at first sight.

1. Introduction

The fact that we are now in 2020 is unimportant: these two books expose the theoretical basis of the matter in a way that is consolidated, and in the ten and more years that have passed nothing has been achieved but some progress in the construction of hardware prototypes. This can be confirmed by reading another very recent, simpler and yet rigorous discussion:

- Bernhardt, Chris, *Quantum Computation for Everyone*, The MIT Press, 2019

which discusses quantum gates and the five fundamental algorithms (referring only by hints to Shor's) in exactly the same way as the previous treatises, and does not contain anything new from the point of view of software development.

Compared to these treatises, our discussion completely lacks both the physical part and the demonstrations of the numerical properties on which quantum algorithms are based, and is aimed at favouring the concrete understanding of the algorithms through implementation; however, the state of things and the potential of quantum computing that are highlighted by our discussion correspond exactly to the conclusions that anyone can draw from a careful reading of those more complex and complete books. Readers are therefore warmly invited to use this book to become familiar with the subject, and then to study the subject in a more abstract and rigorous way in the treatises cited above, which to those who assimilate this book will no longer appear as complex as it happens to those who approach these topics for the first time. The first book to read is Bernhardt's of 2019, which for many readers will have a more than satisfactory theoretical rigor, and also provides a minimal introduction to physics underlying the operation of hardware.

We have no information about the existence of simplified and useful informative works: the simpler books we have consulted are all constructed in a too generic way to allow any understanding of the subject. And in particular we advise readers not to start from quantum programming languages, which as a starting point are incomprehensible, while for the reader who has understood the fundamental quantum algorithms they are an obvious and extremely simple consequence. However, for a simpler and updated discussion oriented to programming languages, you can consult:

- Radovanovic Aleksandar, *Quantum Computing Illustrated*, qpi-book, 2020.

QcNooq project and download of the source code

The source code of the programming examples that are reproduced in the book contains only the instructions necessary for the understanding of the algorithms. We recommend that you read the book carefully a first time without worrying about running the code: if you don't understand what you read in the book, the source code won't help.

Those who wish it could implement their own emulation of the five algorithms using only the code mentioned in the book, just adding the necessary instructions for the output and verification of the results. Anyway, all source code is available in Visual C for Windows. The project is called *QcNooq* and is described in Appendix 1, with instructions for use in Windows and other environments.

Practical information

This book is available in e-book on many e-book stores and also in print format on Amazon. The format was designed to make the book readable even on the small screen of an e-book reader, but with inevitable limitations, so some readers will prefer the paper format.

Notation

The ▶ symbol draws attention to the fact that the following lines contain a definition to remember.

Sometimes in the text there are additional notes and explanations, or parts that can be read quickly by those who already know the details discussed: these parts of the text are in slightly smaller type.

The notation of the source code fragments is that of the C language, of which the simplest constructs similar to those of any other language are used, which are assumed to be known by the reader. However, some explanations are added to clarify what is not entirely obvious. Since the C language is currently used in the discursive parts of the text, when for readability this is appropriate the long names of variables are underlined as in this example: "the result is read in the variable mresult".

The indexes of vectors and matrices throughout the text are indicated in the simplest way given the context, therefore with subscripts when looking at them from a mathematical point of view, and with the notation of C when referring to the implementation. So a vector of real numbers could have the notation v_n or: double v[N], and for an element of it v_j in the first case and v[j] in the second.

For quantum circuits we shall use the notation generally used by all texts, and we shall introduce it at the appropriate moment.

2. Complex numbers

2.1 Arithmetic of complex numbers

Probably all readers of this book remember the basics of complex numbers. Here we recall only those notions that will be used in the implementation of the code to emulate quantum algorithms; the study of quantum physics and quantum computer hardware, on the other hand, would require a complete review, starting with the geometric representation of complex numbers in polar coordinates.

The equation $x = \sqrt{(-1)}$ has no solution, because there is no number that multiplied by itself gives -1. Therefore we define the imaginary unit $i = \sqrt{(-1)}$, which has the following property:

$i^1 = i$;
$i^2 = -1$; (because $\sqrt{(-1)} \times \sqrt{(-1)} = -1$)
$i^3 = -i$; (because $-1 \times i = -i$);
$i^4 = 1$; (because $-\sqrt{(-1)} \times \sqrt{(-1)} = 1$)

and then we start again four by four: $i^5 = i$, $i^6 = -1$,... and so on. If we construct the series by decreasing the exponent, and then dividing by i, we see that:

$i^1 = i$;
$i^0 = 1$;
$i^{-1} = -i$;
$i^{-2} = -1$;
$i^{-3} = i$; etc.

and with this we have also verified that $i^0 = 1$, as for any other number.

A complex number c consists of a real part, which is a real number, and an imaginary part, or a second real number which acts as a multiplier of the imaginary unit. So a complex number is represented as:

$$c = a + bi$$

In the *QcNooq* software and in the source code examples below, we shall use for complex numbers the type qx defined as follows:

```
typedef struct s_qx { double a; double b; } qx;
```

Remember, while reading the following examples, that in C the partial initializations of a structure will fill the uninitialized parts with zeros, and therefore when we want to initialize a qx to the real part only we can use the following declarations:

• complete (correct) initialization with two floating point numbers:

```
qx number = {1.0, 0.0};
```

- initialization of the two members with two integers; conversion to floating point is implied:

```
qx number = {1, 0};
```

- initialization only of member a; b is initialized to 0.0:

```
qx number = {1};
```

Operations with complex numbers

The sum of two complex numbers is a complex number obtained by adding all the corresponding members in the addends, so if $c_0=a_0+b_0i$ and $c_1=a_1+b_1i$, $c_0+c_1=(a_0+a_1)+(b_0+b_1)i$. The code that implements this rule is a function that returns a complex number after adding the members:

```
extern qx qx_add(qx c0, qx c1)
{
qx result;
  result.a = c0.a + c1.a;
  result.b = c0.b + c1.b;
  return result;
}
```

If c=a+bi, −c= −a+−bi, so the code to change the sign of c is:

```
extern qx qx_negate(qx c0)
{
qx result;
  result.a = −c0.a; result.b = −c0.b;
  return result;
}
```

With this we also have the rule for subtraction, since c_0-c_1 is equal to $c_0+(-c_1)$.

The multiplication of two numbers c_0 and c_1 is done by applying the formula:

$$c_0 \times c_1 = (a_0 \times a_1 - b_0 \times b_1) + (a_0 \times b_1 + a_1 \times b_0)i$$

and the corresponding code is:

```
extern qx qx_mul(qx c0, qx c1)
{
qx result;
  result.a = (c0.a * c1.a) − (c0.b * c1.b);
  result.b = (c0.a * c1.b) + (c1.a * c0.b);
  return result;
}
```

▶ The MODULUS of a complex number is indicated with the notation $|c|$ and if $c=a+bi$ the definition of the modulus $|c|$ is: $|c| = \sqrt{(a^2 + b^2)}$. The modulus is a real number, not a complex one. Often we shall use the *modulus squared* quantity, which is: $|c|^2 = (a^2+b^2)$, and which obviously is also real. The code that calculates the modulus squared is:

```
extern double qx_modulus_squared (qx c1)
{
// modulus squared:
double result = (c1.a * c1.a)+(c1.b * c1.b);
  return result;
}
```

The formula for dividing two complex numbers requires the modulus squared of the divisor and is as follows:

$$c_0 / c_1 = ((a_0a_1+b_0b_1) / |c_1|^2) + ((a_1b_0-a_0b_1) / |c_1|^2)i.$$

Obviously the operation is not defined if the modulus of the divisor is zero, and for this reason the corresponding code is in a function where we do not return the complex result, but the status of the operation, which fails if divisor is zero. The result of the operation is assigned to a complex variable of type qx of which we pass the address &resp:

```
extern BOOL qx_div(qx c0, qx c1, qx *resp)
{
// modulus squared of divisor:
double ms = (c1.a * c1.a)+(c1.b * c1.b);
  // we cannot divide by zero:
  if (ms == 0) return FALSE;
  resp->a = ((c0.a * c1.a) + (c0.b * c1.b))/(ms);
  resp->b = ((c1.a * c0.b) - (c0.a * c1.b))/(ms);
  return TRUE;
}
```

Calling this function would be implemented for example like this:

```
qx c0, c1, division;
c0.a = xxxx; // assign values to c0 and c1
if ( qx_div(co, c1, &division) == TRUE )
{
  ...; // Successful call, continue program
}
else
{
  ...; // Unsuccessful call, signal error
}
```

▶ The CONJUGATE of a complex number c is the complex number $c^{conjugate}$ in which only the imaginary part changes sign. So if c=a+bi, $c^{conjugate}$=a–bi:

```
extern qx qx_conjugate(qx c0)
{
qx result;
  result.a = c0.a;  result.b = -c0.b;
  return result;
}
```

For the purpose of our discussion, all that is needed is these few notions.

3. Operations on vectors and matrices of complex numbers

Why did we introduce complex numbers? The reason is that quantum physics uses complex numbers, rather than real, to express the probability of certain state changes of its objects.

We must consider this as a choice introduced by physicists for reasons of expediency, without needing to ask ourselves why, and we must take into account only the difference with the probabilities expressed by means of real numbers. When the probabilities of the different outcomes of a phenomenon are expressed in real numbers, the sum of the probabilities of the different possible outcomes is required to be 1. So if we have four marbles, two of which are green, one red and one blue, we shall say that by extracting one randomly the probability of extracting green is 0.5, that of extracting red is 0.25, that of extracting blue is also 0.25, and the sum of the probabilities is 1.0. If we express probabilities with complex numbers, that is, with pairs of real numbers coordinated according to the rules of complex number arithmetic, as the quantum study of certain subatomic phenomena has chosen to do, then the requirement becomes that not the simple sum, but the sum of the moduli squared $|c|^2$ of the probabilities of the outcome of an event is equal to 1. So, when we are dealing with a phenomenon that has equal probability of ending in state A or in state B, we shall say that states A and B have not 0.5 probability, as would be the case if we were using real probabilities, but they each have probability equal to $1/\sqrt{2}$. In fact, this satisfies the requirement that the sum of the moduli squared is 1, because $(1/\sqrt{2})^2+(1/\sqrt{2})^2 = 1/2+1/2 = 1$. Let us not ask why: let us consider all of this an alternative convention to that applied when real probabilities are preferred, and everything will work equally, as long as we always respect the logical consequences of this convention applied uniquely.

In the following we shall perform operations on vectors (arrays) and on matrices of complex numbers by applying the appropriate rules. We shall define some methods to perform certain operations, of which the most common will be the multiplication of a matrix by a vector, and it may happen that the vectors and matrices on which we shall operate do not contain complex numbers, but real numbers, or even integers or simple boolean values. This does not matter: we can always represent any kind of data with our type qx, corresponding to a+bi, because when b is equal to 0, all the implemented functions will work equally by treating only the real part of the numbers. Let us go back above to see the rules for multiplying and dividing complex numbers: if b=0, in the case of multiplication the rule does nothing but multiply the real parts, and in the case of division it executes $c_0/c_1 = ((a_0 a_1)/a_1^2)$, i.e. a_0/a_1 with a redundancy which is irrelevant for the final result. It is clear that if we were to write software for practical purposes that would perform millions of multiplications and divisions, it would be worthwhile to optimize the cases and not execute the functions for qx complex parameters when not necessary. But if the purpose is only to understand the logic of quantum algorithms, for simplicity we can deal with all kinds of numbers with the operations of complex numbers, and this is what we shall do next.

As for the notation, in the following all the functions that perform operations on vectors and matrices of complex numbers will have as parameters:

- the dimensions of the input vectors or matrices, as appropriate;
- the base addresses of the input vectors or matrices;
- the base address of the resulting vector or matrix, which must be allocated by the calling function and must have the necessary size.

So the parameters will always have the type qx *, pointer to qx, and in the case of matrices the call will require explicit casting to respect the prototype.

For example, the following elementary function changes the sign to all elements of a matrix and copies it into the matrix that is supposed to be allocated as <u>mresult</u>:

```
extern void qx_matrix_negate(int m, int n, qx *m0,
 qx *mresult)
{
int j,k;
  for (j = 0; j < m; ++j) {
    for (k = 0; k < n; ++k) {
      mresult[(j*n)+k] = qx_negate(m0[(j*n)+k]);
    }
  }
}
```

If we were to apply this to a matrix of dimension [3][4], we should proceed as follows:

```
// matrix to be modified, to be initialized
// with the needed values:
qx matrix[3][4];
```

```
// matrix that receives the result of the change
// of sign:
qx matrix_minus[3][4];
// the first two parameters give the function
// the dimensions of the matrix
// the other two parameters give the base
// address of the two input and output matrices:
// notice the necessary cast to the type
// "pointer to qx":
qx_matrix_negate(3,4, (qx *)matrix, (qx
 *)matrix_minus);
```

All functions are written like the one in this example, considering the matrices in the parameters as vectors of one dimension and then explicitly developing the calculation of the index of the corresponding row and column of the element on which to operate. If we were to develop software with more complex application purposes, it would be appropriate to introduce controls on the size of the input and output elements.

The convention is that of the C language, for which if the size of a vector is N, its elements are addressed with an index j ranging from 0 to N−1. All indices are assumed to start from zero and not from one.

For readers who do not find perfectly clear the implementation of qx_matrix_negate().

Readers who are experienced only with the simplest programming languages may find it difficult to understand the qx_matrix_negate() function described above. The following explanation applies to all other similar functions below.

In programming languages we can declare matrices of two or more dimensions, such as m[2][3], m[2][3][6], etc.; but in any case the matrix will be represented as a sequence of objects in a linear memory segment which will have a base address and increasing addresses. The first element of the matrix will have the same address which is considered the address of the overall matrix. So for example the matrix char m[3][2] will be represented in memory as follows:

element:	m[0][0]	m[0][1]	m[1][0]	m[1][1]	m[2][0]	m[2][1]
address:	base+0	base+1	base+2	base+3	base+4	base+5

If the matrix has m rows and n columns, the element of row j and column k can be expressed with m[j][k], with $0 \leq j \leq m$ and $0 \leq k \leq n$. But if we want to write functions to perform operations on two-dimensional arrays of any size, the simplest way is to use that of our function. Inside our function we cannot use the expression m[j][k], because we declared to the compiler that the parameters are the base addresses of the input and output arrays without specifying their lengths, and the actual lengths are only passed to the function at runtime. However, to address the element m[j][k] it is sufficient to use the index [(j*n)+k]: the row is j*n, the column is k. Note that ((j*n)+k) must also be multiplied by the length of the objects in the matrix (in our case the length of qx, which is 16 bytes), but this is performed automatically by the compiler, which has been told that the addresses passed as parameters to the function are objects of the type qx, of which the compiler knows the size. Also note that this method is as fast as possible at runtime, and that if we had to write a program that performs millions of operations this method would be preferable to more complex, though perhaps more readable, constructs.

3.1 Vectors

The operations on vectors of complex numbers qx <u>vector</u>[N] which we must take into account are the following:

▶ Addition of two vectors, which is performed simply by adding all the elements members having the same index. The vectors must have the same size, otherwise the operation is not defined:

```
extern void qx_vector_add (int size, qx *v0, qx
 *v1, qx *vresult)
{
int k;
  for (k = 0; k < size; ++k)
  {
   vresult[k] = qx_add(v0[k], v1[k]);
  }
}
```

▶ Negation of a vector, which changes the sign of all elements:

```
extern void qx_vector_negate(int size, qx *v0, qx
 *vresult)
{
int k;
  for (k = 0; k < size; ++k)
  {
   vresult[k] = qx_negate(v0[k]);
  }
}
```

▶ *Scalar* multiplication of a vector by a number, which multiplies all elements by that number. The input parameters are the scalar multiplier c0 and the vector v0:

```
extern void qx_vector_smul (int size, qx c0, qx
 *v0, qx *vresult)
{
```

```
int k;
  for (k = 0; k < size; ++k)
  {
    vresult[k] = qx_mul(c0, v0[k]);
  }
}
```

Often we shall also need to know the sum of the moduli squared of a vector of complex numbers, so our library also contains the following function:

```
extern double qx_vector_moduli_squared_sum (int
 size, qx *v0)
{
double result = 0.0;
int k;
  for (k = 0; k < size; ++k)
  {
    result += qx_modulus_squared(v0[k]);
  }
  return result;
}
```

which adds nothing to what we know so far.

3.2 Matrices

All the examples of algorithms will use two-dimensional matrices, of the type qx matrix[M][N]. For matrices we can execute:

▶ the sum of all members having the same index of matrices of equal size,

▶ the change of sign, and

▶ the multiplication by a scalar.

The code is obvious:

```
extern void qx_matrix_add (int m, int n, qx *m0, qx
 *m1, qx *mresult)
{
int j,k;
  for (j = 0; j < m; ++j) {
    for (k = 0; k < n; ++k)
    {
    mresult[(j*n)+k] = qx_add(m0[(j*n)+k],
      m1[(j*n)+k]);
    }
  }
}
```

```
extern void qx_matrix_negate(int m, int n, qx *m0,
 qx *mresult)
{
int j,k;
  for (j = 0; j < m; ++j) {
    for (k = 0; k < n; ++k)
    {
     mresult[(j*n)+k] = qx_negate(m0[(j*n)+k]);
    }
  }
}
extern void qx_matrix_smul (int m, int n, qx c0, qx
 *m0, qx *mresult)
{
int j,k;
  for (j = 0; j < m; ++j) {
    for (k = 0; k < n; ++k)
    {
     mresult[(j*n)+k] = qx_mul(c0, m0[(j*n)+k]);
    }
  }
}
```

In addition to the above, the following operations are defined on a matrix:

▶ TRANSPOSE (symbol A^T): given A[m][n], A^T[m][n] is the matrix in which each element A[j][k] is moved to A^T[k][j]. The function must have separate output from the input, because if it operated directly on the input, while proceeding in the loop the original data would be gradually replaced and as the operation progresses part of the input elements would no longer be available:

```
extern void qx_matrix_transpose (int m, int n, qx
 *m0, qx *mresult)
{
int j,k;
  for (j = 0; j < m; ++j) {
    for (k = 0; k < n; ++k)
    {
     mresult[(k*m)+j] = m0[(j*n)+k];
    }
  }
}
```

▶ CONJUGATE (symbol $A^{conjugate}$): given A[m][n], $A^{conjugate}$[m][n] is the matrix in which each complex element [j][k] is replaced by the conjugate, i.e. the complex number in which the imaginary part changes sign. It is obvious that if the numbers are real, the conjugation does not change anything. The function, if desired, could directly modify the input, but for homogeneity we always build the result in a separate memory area:

```
extern void qx_matrix_conjugate (int m, int n, qx
 *m0, qx *mresult)
{
int j,k;
  for (j = 0;  j < m;  ++j) {
    for (k = 0;  k < n;  ++k)
    {
      mresult[(j*n)+k] = qx_conjugate(m0[(j*n)+k]);
    }
  }
}
```

▶ ADJOINT (also called DAGGER, symbol A^+): given A[m][n], A^+[m][n] is the transposed and conjugated matrix. Therefore:

```
extern void qx_matrix_adjoint (int m, int n, qx
 *m0, qx *mresult)
{
int j,k;
  for (j = 0;  j < m;  ++j) {
    for (k = 0;  k < n;  ++k)
    {
      mresult[(k*m)+j] = qx_conjugate(m0[(j*n)+k]);
    }
  }
}
```

▶ The multiplication of two matrices (symbol *) is defined only if they have a common dimension (the number of columns of the first must be equal to the number of rows of the second one). If we have A[m][n] and B[n][p], multiplying A*B gives a matrix C[m][p]. Using this rule we can also multiply a vector by a matrix obtaining a new vector. In fact the vector A[n] is equivalent to a matrix A[1][n] and by executing A[1][n] * B[n][p] the result is a vector C[1][p].

For the multiplication of two or more matrices, let us always recall in the following that A*(B*C) = (A*B)*C holds, while in general A*B = B*A DOES NOT HOLD.

To perform the multiplication A[m][n] * B[n][p] in general, we have to construct the matrix C[m][p] and then assign to each element C[j][k] the sum of the products of each element of row [j] of matrix A by column [k] of matrix B. So the general function, usable for vectors and matrices, is:

```
extern void qx_matrix_mmul(int m, int n, int p, qx
 *m0, qx *m1, qx *mresult)
{
 // a complex number initialized to zero
 qx qx0 = {0,0};
 qx element;
 int i,j,k;
 for (j = 0; j < m; ++j)
 {
   // we must compose the matrix m,p
   for (k = 0; k < p; ++k)
   {
    mresult[(j*p)+k] = qx0;
    // Columns in the first must be equal to rows
    // in the second - parameter n
    for (i = 0; i < n; ++i) {
      // every element contains the summation of
      // the elements i
      // of the row in m0 (j row) multiplied by
      // the element i
      // of the same column in m1 (j column)
      element = qx_mul(m0[(j*n)+i], m1[(i*p)+k]);
      mresult[(j*p)+k] = qx_add(mresult[(j*p)+k],
       element);
    }
   }
 }
}
```

To understand the application examples below, sometimes during the reading it will be necessary to perform multiplications of small vectors or matrices by mind or by hand, so pay attention to the scheme of the procedure. If we have a matrix A[2][2] and another B[2][3], to execute A*B we must allocate the matrix C[2][3] and then populate it in this way:

	0	1	2
0	A[0][0]*B[0][0]+ A[0][1]*B[1][0]	A[0][0]*B[0][1]+ A[0][1]*B[1][1]	A[0][0]*B[0][2]+ A[0][1]*B[1][2]
1	A[1][0]*B[0][0]+ A[1][1]*B[1][0]	A[1][0]*B[0][1]+ A[1][1]*B[1][1]	A[1][0]*B[0][2]+ A[1][1]*B[1][2]

If we have a vector A[2] (i.e. A[1][2]) and a matrix B[2][3], to execute A*B we must allocate the vector C[3] (i.e. C[1][3]) and then populate it in this way:

3. Operations on vectors and matrices of complex numbers

	0	1	2
0	A[0]*B[0][0]+ A[1]*B[1][0]	A[0]*B[0][1]+ A[1]*B[1][1]	A[0]*B[0][2]+ A[1]*B[1][2]

We shall see below that the multiplication of a square matrix by a vector is a fundamental operation in quantum algorithms. Let us notice that the multiplication of one vector by another requires that they have the same length and that we consider one of them horizontal and the other vertical, and the result is a scalar. In fact, to multiply A[N] by B[N] we must consider them as two matrices A[1][N] and B[N][1], and the result is a matrix C[1][1], that is a simple complex scalar.

The multiplication A*B is not commutative, so as we have already said in general it does not hold A*B = B*A. But remember that it holds:

$$(A*B)^+ = (B^+ * A^+).$$

In the *QcNooq* project you can find some examples of multiplication (*QcNooq* 3.A and 3.B).

Some definitions concerning the square matrices (with M=N) are indispensable.

▶ The IDENTITY MATRIX I_n is the square matrix of dimension N where the elements in which j = k have value 1, and those where j ≠ k have value 0. So for example the matrix I_3 is:

1	0	0
0	1	0
0	0	1

and for a square matrix A[n][n] we have the property:

$$A*I_n = A = I_n*A.$$

▶ A square matrix A of dimension [n] is INVERTIBLE if exists a matrix A^{-1} such that $A*A^{-1} = A^{-1}*A = I_n$.

▶ A square matrix U of dimension [n] is UNITARY if $U * U^+ = U^+ * U = I_n$.

Unitary matrices will be fundamental in the following. The code that tests if a matrix is unitary is the following. Here, for the first time, the code is not immediate because to know if a matrix U is unitary, it is necessary to develop the ADJOINT U^+ (transposed and conjugated), perform the multiplication $U*U^+$ and compare all the members. Multiplication is developed internally to the function but is not conserved. To compare two complex numbers we need to use a method which is: qx_complex_equal_enough(). This is the general function:

```c
extern BOOL qx_matrix_is_unitary(int m, qx *m0)
{
qx qx0 = {0.0,0.0};
qx qx1 = {1.0,0.0};
qx item1, total_sum;
qx element;
int i, j, k;
int n = m, p = m; // for readability
  for (j = 0; j < m; ++j) {
    for (k = 0; k < p; ++k) // compose matrix m, p
    {
     total_sum = qx0;
     // Columns in the first must be equal to
     // rows in the second:
     // parameter n
     for (i = 0; i < n; ++i)
     {
      // every member contains the summation
      // of element i
      // of the row in m0 (j row) multiplied by
      // the element i of the same
      // column in m1 (j column)
      // this is to take, but conjugated:
      item1 = qx_conjugate (m0[(k*p)+i]);
      element = qx_mul(m0[(j*n)+i], item1);
      total_sum = qx_add(total_sum, element);
     }
     if (j == k)
     {
      if (! qx_complex_equal_enough(total_sum,qx1))
        return FALSE;
     }
     else
     {
      if (! qx_complex_equal_enough(total_sum,qx0))
        return FALSE;
     }
    }
  }
  return TRUE;
}
```

As an example, let us note that the following matrix U[3][3] is unitary:

3. Operations on vectors and matrices of complex numbers

$\cos\theta$	$-\sin\theta$	0
$\sin\theta$	$\cos\theta$	0
0	0	1

Since the elements are all real, to obtain U^+ it is only necessary to carry out the transposition obtaining:

$\cos\theta$	$\sin\theta$	0
$-\sin\theta$	$\cos\theta$	0
0	0	1

and the multiplication $U*U^+$ gives an identity matrix, because developing it we have:

$\sin^2\theta+\cos^2\theta$	$\sin\theta\times\cos\theta - \sin\theta\times\cos\theta$	0
$\sin\theta\times\cos\theta - \sin\theta\times\cos\theta$	$\sin^2\theta+\cos^2\theta$	0
0	0	1

Recalling that $\sin^2\theta + \cos^2\theta = 1$, we see that the values of the members where $j = k$ are equal to 1, and the others to 0. In the *QcNooq* project point 3.C we can find the verification using the qx_matrix_is_unitary() function.

A detail concerning the implementation of what we are building concerns the function:

```
BOOL qx_complex_equal_enough (qx c0, qx c1).
```

The type qx is a structure, and therefore the expression:

$$\text{if } (c0 == c1)$$

it is not defined, and the compiler would reject it. To compare two complex numbers, the trivial implementation would be:

$$\text{if } (c0.a == c1.a \ \&\& \ c0.b == c1.b),$$

but if we really want to execute the code with numerical examples, we must take into account the approximation of the floating point calculations, which will surely manifest itself by performing multiplications and divisions and then new multiplications on the same numbers. That is, by multiplying a double floating point number by a given factor, then dividing it by the same factor, it can happen and will happen that the number obtained differs from the initial one by a factor whose order of magnitude can be around 10^{-15}. Therefore we need to define a precision threshold that is expected from our floating point operations, and implement the equality test of two complex numbers in this way:

```
#define QX_DOUBLE_PRECISION (1.0e-12)
// also (1.0e-14) could work
extern BOOL qx_complex_equal_enough (qx c0, qx c1)
{
```

```
qx diffe;
  diffe.a = c0.a - c1.a; diffe.b = c0.b - c1.b;
  if (diffe.a < - QX_DOUBLE_PRECISION || diffe.a >
   QX_DOUBLE_PRECISION)
    return FALSE;
  if (diffe.b < - QX_DOUBLE_PRECISION || diffe.b >
   QX_DOUBLE_PRECISION)
    return FALSE;
return TRUE;
}
```

▶ A square matrix A is HERMITIAN if $A^+ = A$. The verification is simple, each element A[j][k] must be equal to the conjugate of A[k][j]:

```
extern BOOL qx_matrix_is_hermitian(int m, qx *m0)
{
int j, k;
  for (j = 0; j < m; ++j)
  {
    for (k = 0; k < m; ++k) {
      if (k == j) continue;
      if (! qx_complex_equal_enough(m0[(k*m)+j],
       qx_conjugate(m0[(j*m)+k])))
        return FALSE;
    }
  }
  return TRUE;
}
```

In the *QcNooq* project point 3.D you can find the verification using the qx_matrix_is_hermitian() function. Notice that a square matrix can be unitary and/or Hermitian. If a matrix is both unitary and Hermitian, then by executing twice the product of the matrix by a vector, the vector returns to its original state: A*A*V = V. In *QcNooq* 3.D there is a numerical example (where the approximation of the floating point calculations can be observed).

▶ TENSOR PRODUCT. An operation that will be performed frequently is the tensor product, which is represented by the symbol $\otimes$. If we have a matrix m0[M][N] and a matrix m1[P][Q], to perform the tensor product m0 $\otimes$ m1 we shall construct a matrix mresult[M*P][N*Q] by replicating M*N times the first matrix and then replacing each member of it with a matrix of dimensions [P][Q] in which we assign to each element the member of the first factor multiplied by the corresponding member of the second.

For example, if m0[2][2] is:

3. Operations on vectors and matrices of complex numbers

a	b
c	d

and m1[2][3] is:

e	f	g
i	j	k

the tensor product m0 $\otimes$ m1 is the following matrix <u>mr</u>[4][6], in which, as can be seen, each element of m0 is replaced by the product of itself for the whole m1:

a×e	a×f	a×g		b×e	b×f	b×g
a×i	a×j	a×k		b×i	b×j	b×k
c×e	c×f	c×g		d×e	d×f	d×g
c×i	c×j	c×k		d×i	d×j	d×k

The algorithm is as follows, and as you can see M×N×P×Q multiplications are performed (in the case of the example above, 2×2×2×3 = 24):

```
extern void qx_matrix_tensor_product(int m, int n,
 int p, int q, qx *m0, qx *m1, qx *mresult)
{
int j,k, a,b, row,col;
  // the destination matrix has dimensions m * p,
  // n * q
  // run through m0 on both dimensions
  for (j = 0; j < m; ++j)
  {
    for (k = 0; k < n; ++k)
    {
      // run through m1 on both dimensions
      for (a = 0; a < p; ++a) {
        for (b = 0; b < q; ++b)
        {
          // indexes in the destination matrix:
          row = a +(j*p);
          col = b +(k*q);
          mresult[row*(n*q) + col] = qx_mul(m0[j*n+k],
            m1[a*q+b]);
        }
      }
    }
  }
}
```

▶ INNER PRODUCT. The inner product is an operation on vectors of equal length which is represented with the symbol $\langle v_0, v_1 \rangle$ and returns a scalar equal to the sum of the products of the values v0[k]*v1[k]. The inner product of vectors of complex numbers requires multiplying the conjugate of the elements v0[k] by v1[k], and therefore the generalized function is the following, which runs through the vectors, calculates the conjugate of v0 and accumulates the sum of the products:

```
extern qx qx_vector_conjugate_and_inner_product(int
  size, qx *v0, qx *v1)
{
qx vx, cresult = {0,0};
int k;
  for (k = 0; k < size; ++k)
  {
    vx = qx_conjugate(v0[k]);
    vx = qx_mul(vx,v1[k]);
    cresult = qx_add(cresult,vx);
  }
  return cresult;
}
```

Given the definition of the conjugate, if the imaginary part is zero qx_conjugate() has no effect. To test the function, see *QcNooq* 3.F.

A remarkable case of inner product is that on bit vectors. If the input data are bit vectors, the resulting scalar must itself be a bit. So the result of the generalized routine should be corrected by taking the remainder of its integer division by two. In fact, if the two bit vectors were v0=[101] and v1=[101], $\langle v_0, v_1 \rangle$ would give: $1\times1+0\times0+1\times1 = 2$. But 2 is not a value for a bit, so the value to assume would be 2%2=0. In other words, the inner product on bit vectors is the parity of the number of cases in which (v0[k]==1 && v1[k]==1). Since in one of the quantum algorithms we shall use the inner product of small bit vectors, it is also useful to define a function to calculate the inner product on bits when the bit vectors are represented as unsigned int (therefore vectors of 32 or 64 bits, according to the implementation), which is:

```
extern char qx_bit_inner_product(int size, unsigned
  int v0, unsigned int v1)
{
unsigned int vr, test;
int k;
char parity = 0;
  vr = v0 & v1;
  for (test = 1, k = 0; k < size; ++k, test <<= 1)
  {
    if (vr & test) parity = 1-parity;
```

```
    }
  return parity;
}
```

The procedure works like this: a logic AND is performed on the bits of the two numbers (bit vectors) of the input, obtaining $\underline{vr}$. We run through $\underline{vr}$ from the least significant bit, switching parity every time a bit equal to 1 is encountered in $\underline{vr}$. The vector length parameter is used because it will happen that we want to know the inner product of vectors with a length less than the maximum size (vectors of 3 bits, 7 bits, for example, etc.), represented in the less significant bits of the parameters. The function returns the type char because the type bit is not implemented, but strictly speaking it should return a bit. To test the function on bits, cf. *QcNooq* 3.G.

Before continuing to read, familiarize yourself with the previous notions, which will be referred to many times. Make sure you are able to go back and see the definition of these matrix operations when we shall use them later.

3. Operations on vectors and matrices of complex numbers

4. Bits and Qubits

4.1 Basic states and evolution of states

Suppose we have an object that can be in one of n states, two or more. For example, a coin resting on a plane showing heads or tails (one of two states), a sphere that can be in a stable state when it falls into one of the six holes of a billiard table (six possible states), or a chemical reagent that can take a certain color in a finite set of possibilities, or a flag that can point north or south in a magnetic field, and so on. Given n possible states, the physical object in question can be in the state x_0, x_1, ... x_i, ... x_{n-1}. If the state is determined, we can represent the condition of the object with a vector of n numbers where the state x_i in which the object is found has the value 1, while the other possible states have 0. Therefore if, for example, the possible states are four and the object is in the second of them, the vector will be: [0,1,0,0]. A symbol called *ket*, $|x\rangle$, is used to represent states according to this convention:

$|x_0\rangle$ means [1,0, ... 0]

$|x_1\rangle$ means [0,1, ... 0]

$|x_i\rangle$ means [0,0, ... 1, ... 0]

$|x_{n-1}\rangle$ means [0,0, ... 1]

The reader has probably instinctively thought that the vector is a bit vector, but this would not be enough. Suppose we now have not the object in a given state, but a certain probability of finding it in one of the n possible states. The vector then becomes the vector of the probabilities of each of the possible states, which could be expressed by real numbers, but which quantum physics, as we know and for reasons we do not discuss, has chosen to express with complex numbers.

▶ With the notation $|\psi\rangle$ we mean an arbitrary state, i.e. a vector of complex coefficients for n states:

$$|\psi\rangle = c_0|x_0\rangle + c_1|x_1\rangle + ... + c_{n-1}|x_{n-1}\rangle$$

and therefore for us a $|\psi\rangle$ corresponds to a vector of complex numbers qx psi[N]. A $|\psi\rangle$ is called a *superposition* of the base states. The complex coefficients are called *complex amplitudes*, and this denomination of the coefficients suggests that physically all this has to do with wave equations: but this concerns the functioning of the hardware, and as always we ignore it. We just need to know that we shall now have to deal with a machine that allows us to do the following basic operations on a certain physical object (the machine will obviously be the circuitry of a quantum computer, which we consider as a theoretical machine, considering only the logic of its operation):

- put the object in a given initial state, which will be expressed with a $|x_i\rangle$;

- modify the object by acting on it with a physical action of some kind (shaking the system, heating it, investing it with electromagnetic frequencies, whatever kind of physical action) in such a way that there is no longer a determined state $|x_i\rangle$, but there are certain probabilities of finding later the object in one of the n possible states: $|x_i\rangle$ is replaced by a $|\psi\rangle$;

- finally, measure the state of the object, that is, detect a new state after having acted on the object, which will be a state $|x_k\rangle$ equal to or different from $|x_i\rangle$. In quantum phenomena, measurement has a special property: it in turn modifies, with a physical action, the superposed state $|\psi\rangle$ and returns a value $|x_k\rangle$ of only one bit. After measurement, it is no longer possible to return to the state $|\psi\rangle$.

The process is described with a fairly exact simile by the simple example of the toss of a coin:

- before being tossed, the coin rests on a solid surface and shows heads or tails, and therefore is in a determined state $|x_i\rangle$ between two possible ones;

- while the coin is in the air, heads and tails have probability 0.5; therefore $|x_i\rangle$ is replaced by $|\psi\rangle = 0.5|x_0\rangle+0.5|x_1\rangle$ (or better $(1/\sqrt{2})|x_0\rangle + (1/\sqrt{2})|x_1\rangle$, as a consequence of what we have said about the total probability at the beginning of chapter 3);

- when the coin falls on a plane, it returns to show heads or tails, and the probability vector $|\psi\rangle$ no longer exists. The strong deceleration that occurs when encountering the plane corresponds to the measurement operation: it hits the system with a violent action that radically changes its state, so that subsequent operations on the vector $|\psi\rangle$ cannot be performed.

The actions performed on the system can be more than one. If the system is in an initial state $|x_i\rangle$, we can act a first time and have, for example, $|\psi_0\rangle = (1/\sqrt{2})|x_0\rangle + (1/\sqrt{2})|x_1\rangle$, then act a second time with a physical operation that increases the probability of x_0 decreasing that of x_1 and obtain for example $|\psi_1\rangle = (\sqrt{3}/\sqrt{4})|x_0\rangle + (1/\sqrt{4})|x_1\rangle$, and so on. The measurement will bring the system back to a certain state $|x_i\rangle$

and does not allow the execution of further transformations of the intermediate states $|\psi_n\rangle$. One can only undertake a new sequence of operations starting from the final determined state.

Thanks to this we begin to glimpse what quantum computation consists of: if we know that a given action has given known probabilities of transforming an initial state into a final one, the physical execution of the action on an object in a known initial state gives an output that is equivalent to, or begins to resemble, the result of a calculation.

Before the final measurement, that is, before the final physical action that detects the state of the object after the previous actions to which it was exposed, each state x_i has the probability:

$$p_i = |c_i|^2 / \||\psi\rangle|^2$$

which we can calculate with our functions:

```
double probability;
qx ci = ....;
qx psi[N] = { .... };
probability = qx_modulus_squared(ci) /
 qx_vector_moduli_squared_sum(N, psi);
```

Given the definition, we have $0 \leq p_i \leq 1$. The probability reduced to a real number by squaring behaves as commonly happens with real probabilities.

Since we shall later emulate the execution of quantum algorithms, which end up with a measurement, we need a function that given a superposition $|\psi\rangle$ returns a state in such a way that by executing the function a large number of times the resulting states are distributed according to the probabilities expressed in $|\psi\rangle$. We must therefore see how the software emulation of the measurement operation can be implemented.

Suppose we have four possible states and a superposition $|\psi\rangle$ which has the following probabilities (we omit to assign the complex part for simplicity):

$$qx \; v0[4] = \{\{2,0\}, \{0,0\}, \{3,0\}, \{1,0\}\};$$

therefore:

$$\||\psi\rangle|^2 = 2\times2+0+3\times3+1 = 14.$$

The real probabilities are $\{4/14, 0, 9/14, 1/14\}$. To extract random states with corresponding distribution, we must imagine arranging the data on a line with intervals equal to the real probability of each possible state, and therefore in our case we would have:

x_0 index from 0 to 3	x_1	x_2 index from 4 to 12	x_3 index 13
└─┴─┴─┴─┘		└─┴─┴─┴─┴─┴─┴─┴─┘	└─┘

Here x_1 does not match any segment because x_1 has probability 0. Now to return a state we need to generate a random number between 0 and 13, find which segment it falls into, and return the corresponding extracted state $|x_i\rangle$. The function that implements this constructs a binary vector of zeros, with a single value = 1 in correspondence with the extracted case. If the measurement is successful, the function returns TRUE and constructs the binary vector corresponding to $|x_i\rangle$, while it returns FALSE if the measurement fails for any error in the input data. We use qx_double_equal_enough() to correct the approximation of the floating point calculations, and it is assumed that we have a qx_random() function that returns a random integer r with $0 \leq r \leq$ QX_RANDOM_MAX, where QX_RANDOM_MAX is a number large enough for our experiments. In input there are the size and the vector in input, and the space to construct the vector in output (which is a vector of complex numbers for homogeneity, but which could be a byte or a bit vector):

```
extern BOOL qx_state_measurement (int size, qx *v0,
 qx *mresult)
{
double total_probability;
double *probabilities;
int k, resindex;
int random_extracted;
  // let us allocate a temporary buffer for real
  // probabilities corresponding to complex input
  probabilities = (double *)malloc(size *
   sizeof(double));
  total_probability =
   qx_vector_moduli_squared_sum(size, v0);
  for (k = 0; k < size; ++k) probabilities[k] =
   qx_modulus_squared(v0[k]);
  // total probability must be meaningful
  if (qx_double_equal_enough (total_probability,
   0.0)) return FALSE;
  // let us put data in the range of our random
  // numbers
  double factor =
   ((double)QX_RANDOM_MAX+1)/total_probability;
  total_probability *= factor;
  for (k = 0; k < size; ++k) probabilities[k] *=
```

```
 factor;
// the items have a segment proportioned to their
// probability
// the whole range will be equal to the range of
// our random numbers
for (k = 1; k < size; ++k) probabilities[k] +=
 probabilities[k-1];
// extract a point in the line:
random_extracted = qx_random();
for (resindex = 0; resindex < size; ++resindex)
{
  if (probabilities[resindex] > random_extracted)
  {
    // if equal to the previous it had probability
    // = 0
    if (resindex > 0 &&
     qx_double_equal_enough(probabilities[resindex]
     , probabilities[resindex-1]))
     continue;
    break;
  }
}
if (resindex < size) // case found
{
  for (k = 0; k < size; ++k)
  {
   mresult[k].a = 0; mresult[k].b = 0;
  }
  mresult[resindex].a = 1;
  free(probabilities);
  return TRUE;
}
free(probabilities);
return FALSE; // failure
}
```

In *QcNooq* at point 4.A we can perform the simulation of the measurement with the vector $|\psi\rangle$ of this example and others. The repeated execution (*QcNooq* 4.B) counts the occurrences of each $|x_i\rangle$ and gives results distributed in proportion to the expected probabilities (for example, by running the test 14000 times it happened to detect $|x_0\rangle$ 3929 times, $|x_2\rangle$ 9070 times and $|x_3\rangle$ 1001 times).

Notice that if a ket $|\psi\rangle$ is multiplied by a scalar, the probabilities remain the same, and therefore a ket can be normalized, making $\||\psi\rangle\|^2$

equal to 1, by means of the operation $|\psi\rangle \,/\, \||\psi\rangle|$. The code snippet is as follows:

```
qx psi[4] = { {5,2}, {7}, {0,4}, {3,2} };
qx psinormal[4];
double msq = qx_vector_moduli_squared_sum(4, psi);
qx inverse_length;
inverse_length.a = 1/sqrt(msq); inverse_length.b =
 0;
// scalar multiplication: we put the factor in a qx
// in order to use our library function valid for
// any type
qx_vector_smul(4, inverse_length, psi, psinormal);
msq = qx_vector_moduli_squared_sum(4, psinormal);
// now output msq and verify that msq == 1.0
```

Therefore, since the probabilities are conserved, the multiplication of a ket by a scalar can always be performed: the physical state represented by the multiplied ket remains the same. Therefore, when needed, normalization can be performed, after which, since $\||\psi\rangle|^2$ becomes equal to 1, the probability of each state simply becomes $p_i = |c_i|^2$.

4.2 Actions on a system

We have said that we must distinguish three phases: first place an object in a given state that is part of a set of possible states, then act on the object in order to change its state, finally "measure" the resulting state. In the second phase, in which we act on the system, we cannot "see" how it is changing: we can know by reasoning that the coin in the air has a 0.5 probability of showing heads when it falls, but we cannot "see" it. In the third phase we "see" how the system has changed through measurement, but measurement is an action that invests the system with an energy of an order of magnitude that modifies it in such a way that the further state is no longer predictable. To get an idea of why, suppose we have to measure the height of a bell tower with an optical instrument: while the bell tower stands where it is, it is subject to constant change due first of all to atmospheric agents, then to the vibrations of the ground due to the circulation of vehicles in the surrounding area, to the light of the sun that hits it, etc. The action of the man who installs a theodolite nearby to intercept the light reflected from the tip of the building can be considered without any influence on the state of the bell tower, and is a measurement that leaves the object in the state it is in. On the other hand, suppose that a person takes two blood samples within a few minutes: it is not impossible that the analysis of the second sample detects some value that is not identical to the first as a result of the fact that the first sample with the needle in the vein was a small violence, to which perhaps the organism has reacted: in this case the measurement does not leave the measured object completely unaltered. All the more reason, the state of an object will be changed if the measurement requires a destructive intervention, with high energy compared to the scale of the system to be measured. Now, in quantum experiments and phenomena the state of subatomic components is detected, and to do this the system is invested with energy whose orders of magnitude are greater than those of the measured object. For example, the position of an electron is revealed by investing the system with electromagnetic frequencies having wavelengths so small that they can interfere with the size of the electron, and therefore of very high energy. Therefore the measurement operations modify the system bringing it into an indeterminable state, and therefore the measurement occurs only once and concludes a quantum calculation.

By way of illustration, we add that theoretically, knowing the system and the measurement operation in full, one could think of being able to calculate the state of the system following the measurement operation: but this is not possible on account of the further factor of the uncertainty of the measurements, that follows from the fact that electromagnetic phenomena occur for indivisible discrete quantities, a factor that makes solutionless certain equations that could have a solution if the electromagnetic phenomena were described only by continuous functions: this is the famous principle of uncertainty, or of indeterminacy. It derives from the fact that in phenomena described by wave equations, the product of energy by time is always an integer multiple of Planck's constant. Therefore, in the measurements something similar happens to the case in which a crashed plane carries a very precise clock, but which indicates only hours and minutes: the scrap of the clock will indicate the hour and minute of the impact, but seconds will not be known.

In the intermediate stage, before the measurement, the actions that can be performed on a system bringing it into superposition and keeping it in such a condition that it can then be measured, all correspond to *unitary and Hermitian* matrices (defined in section 3.2) that are multiplied by the vector of the initial state of the system: this is a fundamental characteristic of the hardware that comes from quantum physics and that is part of the set of principles which we must accept as given. We must acquire and remember the principle according to which hardware can implement actions corresponding to unitary matrices, so that, assuming a succession of times t_j in which the system is in successive states, we have:

$$|\psi_{t1}\rangle = U|\psi_{t0}\rangle$$

The state at time t_1 is described by the result of multiplying a unitary matrix by the state at time t_0. Note that these operations are reversible: we have seen that by multiplying a unitary Hermitian matrix twice by a vector, the vector returns to its original state. This means that if we apply U again to the result of the first multiplication, the system returns to the state of time t_0.

So the general scheme of the steps of a quantum calculation is:

- initialization of an input vector v_0, putting a physical object in a determined state. On one-bit systems, the vector will have the values $|0\rangle$ or $|1\rangle$, and we shall see shortly how the composition of several bits occurs;

- physical action on the system (such as a coin toss). The physical action is described by a U matrix, which is the function of the probability of the outcome of that physical action. So the physical action is equivalent to the multiplication:

$$U * v_0$$

which transforms v_0 into a vector of complex probabilities. Several operations can be performed successively with the same matrix or with different matrices, and therefore v_0 can be transformed, for example, with:

$$U_a * (U_b * (U_a * v_0));$$

- finally, measurement takes place, which is a non-reversible action and does not correspond to a U matrix.

Before testing all this step by step, however, let us introduce the notion of the qubit.

4.3 Qubit

A bit can represent the state of any physical object that can be in two states (white or black, north and south, etc.), corresponding to 0 and 1. But after placing the object in a unique initial state that can be represented with a single digit 0 or 1, if subsequent actions assign a probability of measuring the final state in state zero and another probability of measuring it in state one, then to represent a bit we need a pair of numbers with which to represent the two probabilities:

state	probability
0	c_0
1	c_1

The two numbers c_0 and c_1 cannot be binary bits, since they must express a probability. They might simply be real, but as we know quantum physics needs to use complex coefficients for probabilities. So a qubit is a vector $|\psi\rangle$ of two complex numbers c_0 and c_1, where $p_0 = |c_0|^2 / \||\psi\rangle|^2$ and $p_1 = |c_1|^2 / \||\psi\rangle|^2$ holds, and where $|\psi\rangle$ can always be normalized obtaining $|c_0|^2 + |c_1|^2 = 1$. As we already know, the reason why it was chosen to represent probabilities with complex numbers and not simply with real numbers lies in the physical characteristics of the hardware, and since we are only interested in the logical structure of the computer we simply have to accept it. The complex representation, however, has the consequence that the probability of a bit must be expressed with two complex numbers and not one, which would be enough if the probability were expressed with real numbers. In fact, knowing c_0 we cannot obtain c_1, because we should find the two components a_1 and b_1 of c_1 by means of the only equation: $a_1^2 + b_1^2 = 1 - |c_0|^2$.

In our examples a qubit therefore corresponds to a vector qx v0[2], which gives a first idea (quite underestimated) of the memory required for the software emulation of quantum algorithms: the information necessary to represent a bit requires at least four numbers of the type float, and therefore 64 bits total, which would give little precision in the calculations, or four numbers of the type double for 128 total bits, improving precision.

A very important clarification, fundamental in order not to misunderstand what follows, is this: when a qubit corresponds to a determined binary state, one of the two coefficients has value 1, the other has value 0. So if the object corresponding to the qubit is in the state corresponding to zero, the representation is this:

state	probability
0	1
1	0

which is equivalent to the expression $|0\rangle$, and means: "state zero is true, state one is false". If the object corresponding to the qubit is in the state corresponding to one, the representation is this:

state	probability
0	0
1	1

which is equivalent to the expression $|1\rangle$, and means: "state zero is false, state one is true". The representation:

state	probability
0	0
1	0

makes no sense, it does not describe any condition of the physical object, and it is not mathematically tractable because $|\psi\rangle|^2$, which is the divisor in the calculation of probability, is equal to zero. Instead the representation:

state	probability
0	1
1	1

would express that states zero and one have equal probability of being measured, and could be normalized by executing $|\psi\rangle/\||\psi\rangle|$, obtaining the equivalent, and preferable representation:

state	probability
0	$1/\sqrt{2}$
1	$1/\sqrt{2}$

Now let us simulate the action on a qubit using a Hermitian and unitary notable matrix, which is the Hadamard matrix:

$1/\sqrt{2}$	$1/\sqrt{2}$
$1/\sqrt{2}$	$-1/\sqrt{2}$

for which we use the symbol [H]. The Hadamard matrix, used as a multiplier of a vector, corresponds to a physical action of some kind (a physical action that can take place inside quantum hardware) with which we perturb the initial state of the system making the probability of measuring it in state 0 or 1 equal: in the elementary simile of the coin, it corresponds to the toss in the air. Let us take into consideration the initial states $|0\rangle$ and $|1\rangle$ of a qubit and act on them by multiplying [H] by the vector twice.

For the state $|0\rangle$:

Step	State 0 of the qubit	State 1 of the qubit	Comment
Initialization	1	0	qubit=$|0\rangle$
[H] *	$1/\sqrt{2}$	$1/\sqrt{2}$	equal probability for 0 and 1
Again [H] *	1	0	reversion of the first multiplication

Let us execute the two multiplications explicitly for clarity. We have:

$$\begin{vmatrix} 1/\sqrt{2} & 1/\sqrt{2} \\ 1/\sqrt{2} & -1/\sqrt{2} \end{vmatrix} * \begin{vmatrix} 1 \\ 0 \end{vmatrix} = \begin{vmatrix} 1/\sqrt{2}*1 + 1/\sqrt{2}*0 \\ 1/\sqrt{2}*1 + -1/\sqrt{2}*0 \end{vmatrix} = \begin{vmatrix} 1/\sqrt{2} \\ 1/\sqrt{2} \end{vmatrix}$$

and

$$\begin{vmatrix} 1/\sqrt{2} & 1/\sqrt{2} \\ 1/\sqrt{2} & -1/\sqrt{2} \end{vmatrix} * \begin{vmatrix} 1/\sqrt{2} \\ 1/\sqrt{2} \end{vmatrix} = \begin{vmatrix} 1/\sqrt{2}*1/\sqrt{2} + 1/\sqrt{2}*1/\sqrt{2} \\ 1/\sqrt{2}*1/\sqrt{2} + -1/\sqrt{2}*1/\sqrt{2} \end{vmatrix} = \begin{vmatrix} 1/2 + 1/2 \\ 1/2 - 1/2 \end{vmatrix} = \begin{vmatrix} 1 \\ 0 \end{vmatrix}$$

For the state $|1\rangle$:

Step	State 0 of the qubit	State 1 of the qubit	Comment
Initialization	0	1	qubit=$|1\rangle$
[H] *	$1/\sqrt{2}$	$-1/\sqrt{2}$	equal probability for 0 and 1
Again [H] *	0	1	reversion of the first multiplication

Let us execute again the two multiplications explicitly. We have:

$$\begin{vmatrix} 1/\sqrt{2} & 1/\sqrt{2} \\ 1/\sqrt{2} & -1/\sqrt{2} \end{vmatrix} * \begin{vmatrix} 0 \\ 1 \end{vmatrix} = \begin{vmatrix} 1/\sqrt{2}*0 + 1/\sqrt{2}*1 \\ 1/\sqrt{2}*0 + -1/\sqrt{2}*1 \end{vmatrix} = \begin{vmatrix} 1/\sqrt{2} \\ -1/\sqrt{2} \end{vmatrix}$$

and

$$\begin{vmatrix} 1/\sqrt{2} & 1/\sqrt{2} \\ 1/\sqrt{2} & -1/\sqrt{2} \end{vmatrix} * \begin{vmatrix} 1/\sqrt{2} \\ -1/\sqrt{2} \end{vmatrix} = \begin{vmatrix} 1/\sqrt{2}*1/\sqrt{2} + 1/\sqrt{2}*-1/\sqrt{2} \\ 1/\sqrt{2}*1/\sqrt{2} + -1/\sqrt{2}*-1/\sqrt{2} \end{vmatrix} = \begin{vmatrix} 1/2 - 1/2 \\ 1/2 + 1/2 \end{vmatrix} = \begin{vmatrix} 0 \\ 1 \end{vmatrix}$$

Observe that after the first multiplication the result uniquely indicates which of the two cases we are dealing with, because there is a difference in sign in the second row. The second multiplication returns the state to the initial state. To emulate this process in *QcNooq* (4.D), we use the call qx_matrix_constant() which performs the initialization of a matrix m[2][2] with certain notable values to each of which corresponds a mnemonic code. The code that performs the steps of the first of the two above tables, for state $|0\rangle$, is the following:

```
qx psi0[2]={{1},{0}}; // initial state of the qubit
qx psi1[2];
qx psi2[2];
qx Hadamard[2][2]; // space for Hadamard matrix
```

```
// initialization of Hadamard matrix:
qx_matrix_constant(QX_M22_HADA, (qx *)Hadamard);
// first action on the initial vector
qx_matrix_mmul(2,2,1, (qx *)Hadamard, (qx *)psi0,
  (qx *)psi1);
// output for result verification ...
// second action on the vector
qx_matrix_mmul(2,2,1, (qx *)Hadamard, (qx *)psi1,
  (qx *)psi2);
// output to verify the result, psi2 must be equal
// to psi0 ...
```

As for qx_matrix_constant (), the code snippet is:

```
case QX_M22_HADA:
double S2I;
  S2I = 1.0/(sqrt(2.0));
  dd[(0*2)+0].a = S2I; dd[(0*2)+1].a = S2I;
  dd[(1*2)+0].a = S2I; dd[(1*2)+1].a = -S2I;
```

Let us always remember that in our software emulation, multiplication has a vector in input and a distinct vector in output for a choice of simplicity. If desired, one could implement the functions that modify directly the input (by allocating the necessary temporary buffers within the functions, and taking into account that generally in emulation the input cannot be modified before having finished all the loops needed for the operation). Our choice has the only aim to simplify the emulation and does not correspond to reality: in quantum hardware, multiplication and measurement consist of physical events that always directly alter the input, i.e. the physical state of the objects representing the input, and therefore in reality only the psi0 vector of our example would undergo successive transformations.

Finally, by executing the test code in *QcNooq* (4.D), observe carefully the values of psi2 after the calculation: the approximation of the floating point calculations is manifested, and if the software were to continue testing the equality of the values of psi2 after further operations, qx_complex_equal_enough() should be used as usual.

4.4 Composition of states

Let us now pass to treat the representation of data in a two-bit system, which we shall call x and y, and therefore let us deal the case in which we have two qubits in input. The further composition, from three qubits onwards, will obviously follow the same criteria. We must take this principle into account: every physical action that transforms x and y affects the overall system in such a way that we do not simply have one probability for the transformation of x and another distinct probability for the transformation of y, but we have a probability for every possible state overall in output. This principle is a consequence of the phenomenon of quantum entanglement, which everyone has at least heard of, but which we shall not consider in depth, like everything concerning the construction of hardware. We only have to accept the idea that actions on a system of N qubits always modify the overall system, never an isolated component, and therefore we must accept the consequence that we can never consider the variables x and y independently of each other. Therefore a system of two qubits must be represented like this:

state of x	state of y	probability
0	0	c_0
0	1	c_1
1	0	c_2
1	1	c_3

But while the intermediate states in superposition have a probability c_n for each element of the vector, the initial states and the measured final states have a single value equal to 1 in the row corresponding to the state of x and y. For example, if we initially have x=0 and y=1, the representation will be:

state of x	state of y	initial state
0	0	0
0	1	1
1	0	0
1	1	0

and if after the measurement we have x=1 and y=1, the representation will be:

state of x	state of y	final state after measurement
0	0	0
0	1	0
1	0	0
1	1	1

and therefore in general we shall have a number of cases (and of rows in the representation) equal to 2 raised to the number of bits. The vector representing the state $|\psi\rangle$ will be a vector qx psi[N], where N = 2 raised to the number of bits, so $N = 2^2 = 4$ for two bits, $N = 2^3 = 8$ for three bits, and so on. Both the state vector that is initialized and the state vector resulting from the measurement must have one and only one value equal to 1, the others to 0. As in the case of the single qubit, a vector like [0101] would represent an intermediate state prior to the measurement and would mean that two cases are equally likely, while the other two cases have zero probability. A vector of zeroes would make no sense.

To compose the states we must use the tensor product, described above, both for the input data and for the unitary functions that act on the states. To execute the sequence which we have performed above (with a single qubit) with two bits x and y, we should create an input vector qx psi0[4] resulting from the tensor product of the two qubits and create a matrix qx Hadamard4[4][4] resulting from the product tensor of the basic Hadamard matrix by itself. We should take the following steps:

- initialize the matrix Hadamard4 = [H] $\otimes$ [H];
- assign a value to qubit x;
- assign a value to qubit y;
- initialize the vector psi0 = [qubit x] $\otimes$ [qubit y]. For the parameters of the tensor product, the two qubits are considered both matrices sized [1][2], and the resulting vector a matrix sized [1][2*2];
- run the multiplication twice and check that the operation is reversible.

The code snippet that emulates the verification for all values of x and y is the following (*QcNooq* 4.E):

```
qx qubit_x[2], qubit_y[2];
qx psi0[4]; // input vector
qx psi1[4]; // result of first product
qx psi2[4]; // result of second product
qx Hadamard2[2][2];
qx Hadamard4[4][4];
int x, y, k;
// create the Hadamard matrix for 2 qubits
qx_matrix_constant(QX_M22_HADA, (qx *)Hadamard2);
// create the Hadamard matrix for 4 qubits
qx_matrix_tensor_product(2,2,2,2, (qx *)Hadamard2,
  (qx *)Hadamard2, (qx *)Hadamard4);
  for (x = 0; x <= 1; ++x)
  {
    // initialize qubit x: zero all, set to 1 the
    // appropriate real component
    for (k = 0; k < 2; ++k) qubit_x[k].a =
    qubit_x[k].b = 0.0;
```

```
  qubit_x[x].a = 1.0;
  for (y = 0; y <= 1; ++y)
  {
    // initialize qubit y: zero all, set to 1 the
    // appropriate real component
    for (k = 0; k < 2; ++k) qubit_y[k].a =
      qubit_y[k].b = 0.0;
    qubit_y[y].a = 1.0;
    // inizialize input vector representing the
    // state of 2 qubits
    qx_matrix_tensor_product(1,2,1,2, qubit_x,
      qubit_y, psi0);
    // execute the products acting on input
    qx_matrix_mmul(4,4,1, (qx *)Hadamard4, (qx
      *)psi0, (qx *)psi1);
    qx_matrix_mmul(4,4,1, (qx *)Hadamard4, (qx
      *)psi1, (qx *)psi2);
    // output psi2 to check that it is equal to
    // psi0 ...
  }
}
```

Observe that to initialize ψ_0 we have executed the tensor product of $|x\rangle$ and $|y\rangle$ in order to act scrupulously according to the definitions. In reality we know that with two variables for the vector ψ_0 the possible values are: [1000], [0100], [0010] and [0001], and therefore we could proceed more quickly to build it: but in this way the emulation program would not reflect the conceptual aspect of the problem.

This would be the evolution of $|\psi\rangle$ in the case $x = |0\rangle$ and $y = |0\rangle$:

Step	**x**	0	0	1	1	
	y	0	1	0	1	
Initialization		1	0	0	0	$x=|0\rangle$, $y=|0\rangle$
[H] *		1/2	1/2	1/2	1/2	equal probability for 4 cases
[H] *		1	0	0	0	reversion of the first multiplication

and these the other three cases:

Step	**x**	0	0	1	1	
	y	0	1	0	1	
Initialization		0	1	0	0	$x=|0\rangle$, $y=|1\rangle$
[H] *		1/2	−1/2	1/2	−1/2	equal probability for 4 cases
[H] *		0	1	0	0	reversion of the first multiplication

Step		**x**	0	0	1	1	
		y	0	1	0	1	
Initialization			0	0	1	0	x=$|1\rangle$, y=$|0\rangle$
[H] *			1/2	1/2	−1/2	−1/2	equal probability for 4 cases
[H] *			0	0	1	0	reversion of the first multiplication

Step		**x**	0	0	1	1	
		y	0	1	0	1	
Initialization			0	0	0	1	x=$|1\rangle$, y=$|1\rangle$
[H] *			1/2	−1/2	−1/2	1/2	equal probability for 4 cases
[H] *			0	0	0	1	reversion of the first multiplication

Let us observe that as in the case of the single qubit, after the first product the state of $|\psi\rangle$ is unique for the four cases, because the values of the amplitudes differ for the sign.

A qubyte is obviously an object comprising eight qubits. At first glance, the reader would probably say that if two complex numbers are needed to represent a qubit, sixteen are needed to represent a qubyte. But now we know that this is not the case: for a composite system we need $2^{\text{number of qubits}}$ complex numbers, and therefore for a qubyte we need $2^8 = 256$. The physical actions on a qubyte initialized with a certain state for the 8 bits do not modify the single bits, but the whole, and the measurement must in turn take place on the whole, and therefore the representation of a qubyte is a vector qx psi[256]:

decimal value	binary value, stat of the bits	complex amplitude
0	00000000	c_0
1	00000001	c_1
	....	
254	11111110	c_{254}
255	11111111	c_{255}

which explains why the idea of the necessary memory commitment that we had at first glance considering the single qubit was erroneous by default. It is easy to calculate that a system of 128 bytes, and therefore 1024 bits, would require 2^{1024} (or approximately 1.7×10^{308}) complex numbers. And it is therefore clear that the emulation of quantum algorithms using traditional computers can only be performed to implement tiny examples for study purposes, and that in the future, when quantum coprocessors will exist, these will only work if they will be able to take input data in the classical binary form, expand them internally to themselves and then return the output in the classical binary form.

By studying quantum algorithms we will see exactly what the practical and technical implications of this combinatorial explosion are. For the moment, we just need to understand that if we have to do the calculations relating to N qubits with a classical computer, we must operate on vectors of the order of magnitude of 2^N complex numbers.

4.5 Measurement and result reading

Measurement, as we have already seen, interferes with the system after the physical action that has been exercised on it, and detects the binary state in which the data finally are. For exercise, let us perform the measurement after a single Hadamard transformation of the 2-qubit system. We must initialize both bits to zero, create the matrix Hadamard4[4], create the vector psi0[4] which represents the initial state, act with Hadamard to assign the same probability to all possible states, perform the measurement, and finally know the x and y value after measurement. The measurement will give different results for each run of the program. The code (which executes only the case x=$|0\rangle$, y=$|0\rangle$) is this (*QcNooq* 4.F):

```
qx qubit_x[2] = {{1}, {0}}; // initial state 0
qx qubit_y[2] = {{1}, {0}};
qx psi0[4];
qx psi1[4];
qx measured[4];
qx Hadamard2[2][2];
qx Hadamard4[4][4];
char measured_x, measured_y;

qx_matrix_constant(QX_M22_HADA, (qx *)Hadamard2);
qx_matrix_tensor_product(2,2,2,2, (qx *)Hadamard2,
  (qx *)Hadamard2, (qx *)Hadamard4);

// inizialize input vector representing the state
// of 2 qubits
qx_matrix_tensor_product(1,2,1,2, qubit_x, qubit_y,
  psi0);

// act with Hadamard
qx_matrix_mmul(4,4,1, (qx *)Hadamard4, (qx *)psi0,
  (qx *)psi1);

// execute measurement and check possible error (no
// measurement if psi1 is entirely zero)
if (qx_state_measurement(4, psi1, measured) ==
  TRUE)
```

```
{
  if (qx_check_measured_state(4, measured) < 0)
  {
   ; // ... output error information
  }
  // get the measured value of variable x
  // (variable 0)
  measured_x = qx_state_variable_binary_value(4,
   measured, 0);
  // get the measured value of variable y
  // (variable 1)
  measured_y = qx_state_variable_binary_value(4,
   measured, 1);
  // output for verification
}
else { ... output error information }
```

We have called two auxiliary functions for emulation in *QcNooq*, which we shall need later, but which add nothing to what we already know about quantum algorithms themselves.

The qx_check_measured_state() function returns a value less than zero if the vector is not a measured state, i.e. not a state where one and only one value is 1 and the others are 0. If the check is successful, the function returns the index of the single value equal to 1 in the measured vector:

```
extern int qx_check_measured_state (int size, qx
 *v0)
{
int k, rv = -1;
qx c0 = {0,0};
qx c1 = {1,0};
  for ( k = 0; k < size; ++k )
  {
    if ( qx_complex_equal_enough(v0[k], c0))
     continue;
    if ( qx_complex_equal_enough(v0[k], c1))
    {
     // value 1 found twice or more
     if ( rv != -1 ) return -1;
     rv = k;
     continue;
    }
    // found a value different than 0 or 1
    return -1;
  }
  return rv;
```

}

The qx_state_variable_binary_value() function is used to know, given a vector resulting from measurement, the value of specified variables. The parameter is the index of the variable that we want to read in the vector, with 0=x, 1=y etc. This function is useful to know the value of a given n^{th} bit by emulating systems with more than 2 or 3 bits, where the reading of the vector $|\psi\rangle$ is not immediate:

```
extern char qx_state_variable_binary_value (int
 size, qx *v0, int n_variable)
{
char result = -1; // mask error result = -1
qx qx_one = {1.0, 0.0}; // 1 constant for test
int k, sz, max_variables;
 // if the variable index is >= the log base 2
 // of the state size, the variable index is
 // illegal
 // calculate log base 2 of size:
 for ( sz = size, max_variables = 0; sz > 1; sz
  >>= 1 )
  {
   ++max_variables;
  }
 if ( n_variable >= max_variables ) return result;
  // error
 n_variable = max_variables - (1+n_variable);
 for ( k = 0; k < size; ++k )
  {
   if ( qx_complex_equal_enough( qx_one, v0[k] ) )
   {
   // set result
   result = (k & (1 << n_variable )) ? 1 : 0;
   return result;
   }
  }
 // if the vector is a state
 // we should never get here
 return result;
}
```

Everything that has been explained in this chapter is strictly indispensable: do not continue reading if any aspect is not perfectly clear to you.

4. Bits and Qubits

5. Quantum gates

5.1 Classical gates

Certainly readers are familiar with the meaning of the more usual logic operators, i.e. gates (NOT, AND, OR, XOR and NAND):

Gate	Input	Output	Symbol in C
NOT	x	1 if x = 0, 0 if x = 1	~
AND	xy	1 if x = 1 and y = 1, else 0	&
OR	xy	0 if x = 0 and y = 0, else 1	|
XOR	xy	1 if only one of them = 1	^
NAND	xy	0 if x = 1 and y = 1, else 1	none

and we assume that the readers of this book know that gates are implemented with simple electronic circuits, the composition of which is the basis of the construction of computers and control circuits. Recall that the possible gates on two bits are sixteen, that AND, OR, XOR and NAND are the most commonly used only for practical reasons, not for any intrinsic reason. Even on a single bit there are two possible gates, one of which is NOT, while the other, the simple affirmation, escapes attention because it leaves the bit unchanged and so is of no use. In the following, when it will be useful to mention the gates with a symbol, we shall use those of the bit operators of the C language, in order to standardize the representation to the program examples. However, NAND does not have a symbol in C.

Moreover, the C language has a distinction between the logic operators in the strict sense on variables and the corresponding operations at the bit level. We shall need this distinction in chapter 6.3 for Simon's algorithm, and it will be recalled there.

We need to introduce a new factor: it is now necessary to express the gates using the data representation used for qubits. Each gate can be represented as a matrix that multiplies a vector $|\psi\rangle$, which remaining in the classical context will be considered a simple vector of Boolean values, and not of complex numbers, but which however will not have just one Boolean value but two, one for the representation of the state $|0\rangle$ (vector [10]) and one for the representation of the state $|1\rangle$ (vector [01]).

Therefore, the NOT gate will be represented with the matrix:

0	1
1	0

because we have for $NOT|0\rangle = |1\rangle$:

0	1
1	0

$*$

1
0

$=$

0
1

and for $NOT|1\rangle = |0\rangle$:

0	1
1	0

$*$

0
1

$=$

1
0

To implement the corresponding code it would be obvious to use the BOOL type, but everything works the same even using the qx type – as we know, the representation in complex numbers is redundant, but it always gives the expected result even in the absence of the imaginary part. Therefore (*QcNooq* 5.A):

```
qx NOT_gate[2][2] = { {{0},{1}},
{{1},{0}} };
qx bit_0[2] = {{1},{0}};
qx bit_1[2] = {{0},{1}};
qx not_bit[2];
// execution of NOT 0:
qx_matrix_mmul(2,2,1, (qx *)NOT_gate, bit_0,
 not_bit);
// execution of NOT 1:
qx_matrix_mmul(2,2,1, (qx *)NOT_gate, bit_1,
 not_bit);
```

The representation of gates on two bits occurs with non-square and non-unitary matrices (we are still in the classical world), and for AND we have:

1	1	1	0
0	0	0	1

In fact, as we know from the definition of AND, $AND|00\rangle$, $AND|01\rangle$ and $AND|10\rangle$ give $|0\rangle$, while $AND|11\rangle$ gives $|1\rangle$. For example, to execute the case $AND|11\rangle$, we must represent the input with the tensor product of the two bits, which gives [0001], and then execute:

1	1	1	0
0	0	0	1

$*$

0
0
0
1

$=$

0
1

To check the AND gate, the code requires attention to the lengths of the input and output vectors and to the parameters. Bits are vectors of two elements, and their tensor product gives phi0[4]. The matrix is AND_gate[2][4]. The product we perform is AND_gate * phi0, so we multiply a matrix sized [2][4] by another matrix sized [4][1], the result has the dimensions [2][1], and is RESULT_phi0[2]. In fact, the

AND operator in input has 2 bits, while in output it has only one. The code is as follows (as usual, the use of the qx type is redundant but without consequences):

```
qx bit_0[2] = {{0},{1}}; // x = |1>
qx bit_1[2] = {{0},{1}}; // y = |1>
qx phi0 [4];
qx RESULT_phi0[2];
qx AND_gate[2][4] = { {{1},{1},{1},{0}},
{{0},{0},{0},{1}} };
int k;
// create phi representing the state of input
qx_matrix_tensor_product(1,2,1,2, bit_0, bit_1,
 phi0);
// execute AND|xy>
qx_matrix_mmul(2,4,1, (qx *)AND, phi0,
 RESULT_phi0);
// get value of result for output
k = qx_state_variable_binary_value(2, RESULT_phi0,
 0);
```

In *QcNooq* 5.B there are routines to check the AND, OR, XOR and NAND gates on the 4 possible inputs. For the NAND gate, we note that the matrix is obtained from the product NOT * AND. In fact NAND|xy⟩ is equivalent to NOT(AND|xy⟩), and we know that the multiplication of matrices has the property: A*(B*C)=(A*B)*C. So NAND can be composed as follows (the multiplication of a matrix [2][2] by a matrix [2][4] gives a result of dimensions [2][4]):

```
qx NOT_gate[2][2] = { {{0},{1}},
{{1},{0}} };
qx AND_gate[2][4] = { {{1},{1},{1},{0}},
{{0},{0},{0},{1}} };
qx NAND_gate[2][4]; // to be built
// build NAND multiplying NOT * AND
qx_matrix_mmul(2,2,4, (qx *)NOT_gate, (qx
 *)AND_gate, (qx *)NAND_gate);
```

Pay close attention to this: we introduced this matrix representation of common gates applicable to two-bit arguments to familiarize ourselves with the representation of data in a quantum computer, but for the reasons that we shall see shortly these gates cannot be implemented in a quantum computer. To avoid misunderstanding, the reader from now on must remember and take into account that a gate like AND does not and cannot exist in a quantum computer.

5.2 Identity gate and reversible gates

There is a gate that in the traditional world does not draw attention on account of its obviousness: the identity I_n, which leaves the input in the state in which it is. The identity matrix on a ket representing a bit, obviously is the negation of the negation, i.e. the affirmation, and is I_2:

1	0
0	1

The identity matrix is essential to create assembled gates. Suppose we want to create an assembled gate that has 2 bits, x and y, in input, and must return |x⟩ negated and |y⟩ unchanged in output. This gate returns NOT|x⟩ and IDENTITY|y⟩, so both in input and output we have a vector phi[4]. To create the operator that performs the desired operation we must construct the compound operator U[4][4] using the tensor product NOT $\otimes$ I_2: then the product U[4][4] * phi0[4] will return a vector phi1[4], which will represent the changed state of the two bits. The matrix of NOT|x⟩, IDENTITY|y⟩ is this (perform the tensor product NOT $\otimes$ I_2 with pencil and paper for exercise):

0	0	1	0
0	0	0	1
1	0	0	0
0	1	0	0

and we can verify it for the 4 possible inputs (see *QcNooq* 5.C):

xy	input	xy in	xy out	column 0 of NOTx IDEy
00	1	00		0
01	0			0
10	0		10	1
11	0			0

xy	input	xy in	xy out	column 1 of NOTx IDEy
00	0			0
01	1	01		0
10	0			0
11	0		11	1

xy	input	xy in	xy out	column 2 of NOTx IDEy
00	0		00	1
01	0			0
10	1	10		0
11	0			0

xy	input	xy in	xy out	column 3 of NOTx IDEy
00	0			0
01	0		01	1
10	0			0
11	1	11		0

Execution in *QcNooq* 5.C with x=|0⟩, y=|1⟩:

```
qx NOT_gate[2][2] = { {{0},{1}},
{{1},{0}} };
qx IDE_gate[2][2] = { {{1},{0}},
{{0},{1}} };
qx NOT_IDE_gate[4][4];
qx bit_0[2] = {{1},{0}}; // |0>
qx bit_1[2] = {{0},{1}}; // |1>
qx phi0 [4];
qx result_phi[4];
// build composed gate
qx_matrix_tensor_product(2,2,2,2, (qx *)NOT_gate,
 (qx *)IDE_gate, (qx *)NOT_IDE_gate);
// create phi representing the state of input:
qx_matrix_tensor_product(1,2,1,2, bit_0, bit_1,
 phi0);
// execute gate:
qx_matrix_mmul(4,4,1, (qx *)NOT_IDE_gate, phi0,
 result_phi);
// output for verification ...
```

The output vector <u>result_phi</u> in this case is [0001], that is |11⟩, that is x =|1⟩, y =|1⟩, as expected.

Let us now observe that the two gates NOT and IDENTITY, and their compositions obtained with the tensor product, are reversible: by executing the gate twice, the input returns to the initial state. On the contrary, the AND, OR, XOR gates are not reversible, because:

- if AND|xy⟩ is false, the initial state is unknown, which can be |00⟩, |01⟩, |10⟩.

- if OR|xy⟩ is true, the initial state is unknown, which can be |01⟩, |10⟩, |11⟩.

- for XOR|xy⟩ we can never go back to the initial state.

and this corresponds to the fact that the matrices of the classical operators are not necessarily square. By our calculations through matrix products, the reversion of AND, OR and XOR could not even be expressed.

The gates used in quantum circuits must be reversible, and correspond to unitary square matrices. We must accept this rule as a fact that comes to us from the outside, like any other physical feature of the hardware. To get an idea of the reason, let us just mention that the reason concerns the energy balance of the system that makes up the hardware. The execution of a non-reversible gate such as AND loses information, because before AND we know the status of two bits and after we only know one bit of the result. Now, it has been shown that with any hardware the loss of information corresponds to a transfer of energy from the physical system to the outside, while the execution of a gate that preserves the information entirely, and therefore preserves the elements with which to implement the reversion, can be energy balanced: given the delicacy of quantum hardware, it is possible to implement only reversible gates.

Reversible gates can be built with basic gate compositions, introducing certain redundancies. The first gate we consider is called *controlled–NOT*: in input it has two bits, in output it also has two bits: one is the first unchanged bit, the other is the result of the XOR of the two input bits:

controlled–NOT	
input	output
$|x\rangle$	$|x\rangle$
$|y\rangle$	$|x^\wedge y\rangle$

therefore we can also write: $[\text{controlled–NOT}]|x,y\rangle = |x,x^\wedge y\rangle$. Applying controlled–NOT twice we have:

input		output		output
$|x\rangle$ $|y\rangle$	[controlled–NOT]	$|x\rangle$ $|x^\wedge y\rangle$	[controlled–NOT]	$|x\rangle$ $|x^\wedge(x^\wedge y)\rangle = |y\rangle$

and therefore we return to the initial state. Controlled–NOT can be obtained as $I_2 \otimes \text{NOT}$, and the matrix is:

1	0	0	0
0	1	0	0
0	0	0	1
0	0	1	0

and we can build it like this:

```
qx IDE_gate[2][2] = { {{1},{0}},
{{0},{1}} };
qx NOT_gate[2][2] = { {{0},{1}},
{{1},{0}} };
qx controlled_NOT_gate[4][4];
// build composed gate
qx_matrix_tensor_product(2,2,2,2, (qx *)IDE_gate,
  (qx *)NOT_gate, (qx *)controlled_NOT_gate);
```

The software in *QcNooq* 5.D applies controlled–NOT for verification of the reversion:

```
void QCF_gate_controlled_NOT()
{
qx IDE_gate[2][2] = { {{1},{0}}, {{0},{1}} };
qx NOT_gate[2][2] = { {{0},{1}}, {{1},{0}} };
qx controlled_NOT_gate[4][4];

// build composed gate
qx_matrix_tensor_product(2,2,2,2, (qx *)IDE_gate,
 (qx *)NOT_gate, (qx *)controlled_NOT_gate );

qx bit_0[2] = {{1},{0}}; // |0>
qx bit_1[2] = {{0},{1}}; // |1>
qx phi0 [4];
qx RESULT_phi[4];
qx RESULT_phi_reverse[4];
qx RESULT_phi_reverse_reverse[4];

// create phi representing the state of input
qx_matrix_tensor_product(1,2,1,2, bit_0, bit_1,
 phi0 );
// execute gate:
qx_matrix_mmul(4,4,1, (qx *)controlled_NOT_gate,
 phi0, RESULT_phi );
// output (0, "Applied Gate controlled-NOT",
// 1,4,RESULT_phi );
qx_matrix_mmul(4,4,1, (qx *)controlled_NOT_gate,
 RESULT_phi, RESULT_phi_reverse );
// output (0, "Applied Gate controlled-NOT First
// reversion", 1,4,RESULT_phi_reverse );
qx_matrix_mmul(4,4,1, (qx *)controlled_NOT_gate,
 RESULT_phi_reverse, RESULT_phi_reverse_reverse );
// output (0, "Applied Gate controlled-NOT Second
// reversion", 1,4,RESULT_phi_reverse_reverse );
}
```

All the rest of this chapter 5 is not necessary for the understanding of the quantum algorithms treated in chapter 6: so now let us quickly mention the other remarkable reversible gates only to complete the discussion and to get an idea of what can be built on the basis of reversible gates. However, do not neglect to read the following carefully, as it serves as an exercise in the typical, and unusual, way of reasoning that we shall have to apply to understand quantum algorithms.

5. Quantum gates

A remarkable gate is the *Toffoli gate*, which operates on three variables:

Toffoli gate	
input	output
$|x\rangle$	$|x\rangle$
$|y\rangle$	$|y\rangle$
$|z\rangle$	$|z^\wedge(x\&y)\rangle$

therefore $[\text{Toffoli}]|x,y,z\rangle = |x, y, z^\wedge(x\&y)\rangle$. The matrix of the Toffoli gate is:

1	0	0	0	0	0	0	0
0	1	0	0	0	0	0	0
0	0	1	0	0	0	0	0
0	0	0	1	0	0	0	0
0	0	0	0	1	0	0	0
0	0	0	0	0	1	0	0
0	0	0	0	0	0	0	1
0	0	0	0	0	0	1	0

The dimension is 8, that is 2^3, since the variables are 3. To construct the Toffoli gate in *QcNooq* (5.E) we have defined a mnemonic and we can execute:

```
qx Toffoli[8][8];
// build composed gate as a constant
qx_matrix_constant(QX_M88_TOFFOLI, (qx *)Toffoli);
```

where the code snippet that initializes the matrix is:

```
case QX_M88_TOFFOLI:
 // Toffoli gate 8 * 8
 memset(dd, 0, 8*8*sizeof(qx) );
 // constant values of Toffoli:
 for ( j = 0; j < 6; ++j ) dd[j*8 + j].a = 1;
 dd[6*8 + 7].a = 1; dd[7*8 + 6].a = 1;
```

Let us observe that this gate has the property of being a universal gate, and using it in a composite way it can be used to construct any gate. In fact:

If $|z\rangle = |0\rangle$, the output is $|0^\wedge(x\&y)\rangle$. But $|0^\wedge a\rangle = |a\rangle$, therefore with $|z\rangle = |0\rangle$ Toffoli is equivalent to $\text{AND}|x,y\rangle$.

If $|z\rangle = |1\rangle$, the output is $|1^\wedge(x\&y)\rangle$. But $|1^\wedge a\rangle = |!a\rangle$, therefore with $|z\rangle = |1\rangle$ Toffoli is equivalent to $\text{NAND}|x,y\rangle$.

If $|x\rangle = |1\rangle$ and $|y\rangle = 1$, the output is $|z^\wedge(1\&1)\rangle$, i.e. $|z^\wedge 1\rangle$, i.e. $|!z\rangle$. Therefore with $|x\rangle = |1\rangle$ and $|y\rangle = 1$ Toffoli is equivalent to $\text{NOT}|z\rangle$.

If $|y\rangle = |1\rangle$, Toffoli is equivalent to $\text{XOR}|x,z\rangle$.

Two Toffoli gates can be used to derive OR from AND by means of the De Morgan's laws, and so on. In this way we get a first idea of the universal potential of quantum gates.

Another remarkable reversible gate is the *Fredkin gate*, which operates on three variables:

Fredkin gate	
input	output
$|x\rangle$	$|x\rangle$
$|y\rangle$	se $|x\rangle = 0$ $|y\rangle$ else $|z\rangle$
$|z\rangle$	se $|x\rangle = 0$ $|z\rangle$ else $|y\rangle$

The Fredkin gate matrix is this:

1	0	0	0	0	0	0	0
0	1	0	0	0	0	0	0
0	0	1	0	0	0	0	0
0	0	0	1	0	0	0	0
0	0	0	0	1	0	0	0
0	0	0	0	0	0	1	0
0	0	0	0	0	1	0	0
0	0	0	0	0	0	0	1

To construct the Fredkin gate in *QcNooq* (5.E) we define a mnemonic and use:

```
qx Fredkin [8][8];
// build composed gate as a constant
qx_matrix_constant(QX_M88_FREDKIN, (qx *) Fredkin);
```

The code to initialize the matrix is obvious. The Fredkin gate is also shown to be universal, and can be used for the composition of any gate.

5.3 Quantum gates

The unitary and reversible operators that can act on qubits are called quantum gates. We have already encountered some gates, or matrices, with these characteristics:

- Identity I_n of N dimensions
- Hadamard H_n of N dimensions
- NOT
- controlled–NOT
- Toffoli
- Fredkin

A final notion, which we shall not need for algorithms, but is essential to understand how a quantum computer can be a universal computer, is this: a theorem is proved which ensures that there are universal sets of quantum basic gates, with the which all the unitary matrices applicable to a quantum input can be composed. One of these sets consists of:

$$\{\text{Hadamard, } R_\theta \text{ with } \theta=\arccos(3/5), I_n, \text{controlled–NOT}\}$$

Of these gates, we do not know R_θ, whose definition is:

$$\begin{array}{|c|c|} \hline 1 & 0 \\ \hline 0 & e^\theta \\ \hline \end{array}$$

When $\theta = \arccos(3/5)$, R_θ is part of the universal set. We have only mentioned this notion to give an idea of how the writing of quantum software will take place: a quantum programming language will give the means to act on the input through compositions of the matrices of the universal set, and in this way will allow the assembly of applications.

6. Quantum Algorithms

In general, quantum algorithms will serve to transform an input by applying a given function and will follow this scheme:

- some qubits are initialized with binary values (classical state), and the initial state of the set of the qubits is represented as a $|\psi\rangle$ of binary values;

- the system is put in superposition by assigning real or complex probabilities different from 0 and 1 to the members of the qubits;

- one or more unitary matrices are defined, which represent the input transformation function;

- we act on the input in superposition by multiplying the matrices representing the function by it one or more times;

- the transformed qubits are measured, and so reduced to binary values.

Let us always remember that an action on an input in software emulation is the execution of a multiplication through a routine, while in the reality of a quantum computer it will consist of a physical event that stimulates and transforms the system in a controlled way: it is the toss into the air of the coin, to resort to the usual elementary simile. So the execution of the multiplication will take place in a single physical event rather than in a repeated loop, and this is the reason of the potential of quantum computing.

A warning for reading: since to express ourselves compactly we use the C language, to correctly express the type corresponding to binary truth values we should use the BOOL type. For simplicity, however, we shall feign that the 'bit' type exists, which obviously cannot have other values than 0 or 1.

6.1 Deutsch's algorithm

Deutsch's algorithm corresponds to the "Hello, World!" program which is usually mentioned at the beginning of books teaching programming in any language. The problem solved by Deutsch's algorithm is of theoretical interest only, and is of such small size as to be surprising that something so complex can be written about it. However, it serves to understand how a problem that a classical computer solves in TWO cycles can be solved by the quantum computer by acting ONCE on the input.

This is the problem. Suppose we have a function func() whose prototype is:

bit func(bit);

So the argument is a bit, the returned value is a bit, and we have these 4 possible cases (that is, the functions corresponding to this prototype are 4):

Input	Output = func(input)			
0	0	0	1	1
1	0	1	0	1
	constant	balanced	balanced	constant

If func(0) == func(1), the function is said *constant*.

If func(0) != func(1), the function is said *balanced*.

And the four possible functions return:

- constant zero
- input
- NOT input
- constant one.

The problem to solve is this: suppose we have a routine that calculates the func function, and that we cannot read either the flowchart or the source code: the func function is a black box. We want to know if the func function is constant or balanced. To get the answer, we have to execute the function twice, with argument 0 and with argument 1. Is it possible to build an algorithm that gives us the answer by acting only once on the input data?

Note this well: in the discussion that follows, it is not literally true that the function func is a black box, because we see its contents very well, and we could not proceed without seeing it. But the problem is: is it possible to answer the question "is the function constant or balanced?" avoiding to execute the function twice, and the whole discussion only serves to illustrate the setup necessary to give this answer.

First, each of the 4 functions <u>func</u> corresponds to a matrix. The cases are:

1) for the constant function which always returns 0:

1	1
0	0

2) for the balanced function that returns the input:

1	0
0	1

3) for the balanced function that returns NOT input:

0	1
1	0

4) for the constant function which always returns 1:

0	0
1	1

It is immediate that these matrices correspond to the definition of the functions, and that they can produce the output by multiplying the function by a bit expressed as $|0\rangle$ or $|1\rangle$ in input. For verification, let us multiply one of the matrices by a state. Let us choose case 3, which returns NOT input, and multiply the matrix by the state $|0\rangle$. The state $|0\rangle$ is the state in which the value $|0\rangle$ has total probability, and therefore corresponds to a vector [1,0]. The multiplication of matrix 3 by $|0\rangle$ is therefore:

0	1		1
1	0	*	0

and let us remember that it is performed with the rule of the multiplication of matrices, constructing an output vector in which each element contains the sum of the products of the values of the rows of the matrix, multiplying every element with index of the column in the matrix equal to the corresponding row of the vector. So the resulting vector is:

output[0] = matrix[0][0]*input[0] + matrix[0][1]*input[1];

output[1] = matrix[1][0]*input[0] + matrix[1][1]*input[1];

so in the chosen case we have:

output[0] = 0*1 + 1*0 = 0;

output[1] = 1*1 + 0*0 = 1;

and therefore the resulting vector is [0,1] which corresponds to the state $|1\rangle$, and therefore to NOT input. For the complete verification of the four matrices, cf. *QcNooq* 6.1.A.

We could not continue now with a quantum algorithm, because two of the four matrices are not unitary, and precisely in the two constant cases the result is not reversible: when the output is constant 0 or 1 we cannot deduce the input. We must therefore expand the matrix with the technique for constructing reversible gates seen in the previous chapter, and construct for each function a matrix which on the input side has all the possible values of input x and output y, and on the output side has the repetition of the input x and the possible values not of f(x), but of y^f(x). That is, we use the properties of the gate controlled–NOT to make the function reversible.

For the function of the first case, where $f(x) = 0$ constant, the matrix is the following:

	00	01	10	11
00	1	0	0	0
01	0	1	0	0
10	0	0	1	0
11	0	0	0	1

In the left column we have the possible cases of x and y, in the upper row the possible cases of x and y^f(x). Let us check step by step that the table is built correctly. Let us develop all the steps and verify that in the matrix representing the function, the values equal to 1 are found in the columns corresponding to the value assumed by x and y^f(x). So for each x and y we shall develop f(x) and y^f(x), and so we can identify which column of the matrix must have the value 1 because it corresponds to x and y^f(x):

	x	y	f(x)	y^f(x)	x, y^f(x)	00	01	10	11
00	0	0	0	0^0=0	00	1			
01	0	1	0	1^0=1	01		1		
10	1	0	0	0^0=0	10			1	
11	1	1	0	1^0=1	11				1

For the function of the second case, where $f(x) = x$, the matrix is the following:

	00	01	10	11
00	1	0	0	0
01	0	1	0	0
10	0	0	0	1
11	0	0	1	0

Verify, with the same technique:

	x	y	f(x)	y^f(x)	x, y^f(x)	00	01	10	11
00	0	0	0	0^0=0	00	1			
01	0	1	0	1^0=1	01		1		
10	1	0	1	0^1=1	11				1
11	1	1	1	1^1=0	10			1	

For the function of the third case, where $f(x) = NOT(x)$, the matrix is the following:

	00	01	10	11
00	0	1	0	0
01	1	0	0	0
10	0	0	1	0
11	0	0	0	1

Verification:

	x	y	f(x)	y^f(x)	x, y^f(x)	00	01	10	11
00	0	0	1	0^1=1	01		1		
01	0	1	1	1^1=0	00	1			
10	1	0	0	0^0=0	10			1	
11	1	1	0	1^0=1	11				1

For the function of the fourth case, where $f(x) = 1$ constant, the matrix is the following:

	00	01	10	11
00	0	1	0	0
01	1	0	0	0
10	0	0	0	1
11	0	0	1	0

Verification:

	x	y	f(x)	y^f(x)	x, y^f(x)	00	01	10	11
00	0	0	1	0^1=1	01		1		
01	0	1	1	1^1=0	00	1			
10	1	0	1	0^1=1	11				1
11	1	1	1	1^1=0	10			1	

Since we have 4 functions and 4 values of $|xy\rangle$, we obviously have 16 total cases. Now let us execute the first of the 16 total cases, applying the function that returns constant zero to the input $|00\rangle$. The vector representing the input is [1000] because the input is $|00\rangle$:

xy	
00	1
01	0
10	0
11	0

and we need to multiply:

1	0	0	0		1		1
0	1	0	0	*	0	=	0
0	0	1	0		0		0
0	0	0	1		0		0

The result is a vector that in the first column replicates x, and in the second column has y^f(x):

x	y^f(x)	
0	**0**	1
0	**1**	0
1	**0**	0
1	**1**	0

So to know f(x) we have to execute (y in input)^(y^f(x) in output), in our case 0^0, which is equal to zero, as expected, since the function returns constant zero. *QcNooq* at point 6.1.C performs all possible cases. The code snippet to run a case is as follows:

```
// initialize the matrix of the constant zero
// function
qx mout0 [4][4] = { {{1},{0},{0},{0}},
 {{0},{1},{0},{0}},  {{0},{0},{1},{0}},
 {{0},{0},{0},{1}},  };
// initialize input
// input with x = 0, y = 0:
x input_00[4] = {{1},{0},{0},{0}};
qx output[4];  // vector for output
// act on the vector executing the multiplication
qx_matrix_mmul(4,4,1,(qx *)mout0, (qx *)input_00,
 output);
// find the value of the second variable in output
// (the index of the variable is 0 for x, 1 for y
char y_xor_fx;
y_xor_fx = qx_state_variable_binary_value(4,
 output, 1);
// remember that in case of an error (non-binary
// status) -1 is returned
if (y_xor_fx < 0)
{
  // ... output software error
}
// fx is (y in input)^(y^f(x) in output), so:
char fx;
fx = 0 ^ y_xor_fx;
// ... display fx to verify that fx corresponds to
// the expected value for the case
```

Now let us go back to the problem to be solved, that of finding a technique to answer the question: "is the function constant or balanced?" executing the function only once. The answer is given by the following quantum circuit applied to input $|01\rangle$. $[U_f]$ is the unitary matrix of the function considered, $[H]$ is the Hadamard gate and $[I]$ the unitary matrix, according to the notation introduced previously. For measurement we shall use the symbol $[M]$. The steps are as follows:

0: initialization of $|\psi 0\rangle$
1: action with Hadamard on x and y
2: action with the U_f function on x and y
3: action with Hadamard on x, and with Identity on y which remains unchanged
4: measurement of x

The steps can be represented in a sequence from left to right as follows:

Step:	0	1	2	3	4
x	$|0\rangle$	[H]		[H]	[M]
y	$|1\rangle$	[H]	$[U_f]$	[I]	
Output:	$|\psi_0\rangle$	$|\psi_1\rangle$	$|\psi_2\rangle$	$|\psi_3\rangle$	

and correspond to these operations, now represented from right to left because the leftmost multiplier is the one that acts later:

$$([H]\otimes[I])\, U_f\, ([H]\otimes[H])\, |0,1\rangle.$$

The corresponding code snippet is as follows. We must initialize U_f (variable <u>mout0</u>) and the input, construct the Hadamard matrix of needed dimension <u>haha</u>[4][4] by means of the <u>Hadamard</u>[2] tensor product by itself and construct the matrix <u>haid</u>[4][4] which executes ($[H]\otimes[I]$) by means of the tensor product of Hadamard and Identity. Then perform the multiplications in sequence:

```
// matrix Uf that given x and y gives x and y^f(x):
qx mout0 [4][4] = { {{1},{0},{0},{0}},
 {{0},{1},{0},{0}}, {{0},{0},{1},{0}},
 {{0},{0},{0},{1}}, };
qx ha[2][2], ide2[2][2], haha[4][4], haid[4][4];
// input with x = 0, y = 1:
qx input_01[4] = {{0},{1},{0},{0}};
// initialize the necessary constants
// Hadamard[2][2]
qx_matrix_constant(QX_M22_HADA, (qx *)ha);
// Identity[2][2]
qx_matrix_constant(QX_M22_IDEN, 1, (qx *)ide2);
// Hadamard for both variables (step 1)
```

```
qx_matrix_tensor_product(2,2,2,2, (qx
 *)ha,(qx *)ha,(qx *)haha);
// Hadamard for x, Identity for y (step 3)
qx_matrix_tensor_product(2,2,2,2, (qx *)ha,(qx
 *)ide2,(qx *)haid);
// data for output of every step
qx phi1[4], phi2[4], phi3[4], measured[4];
// step 1
qx_matrix_mmul(4,4,1,(qx *)haha, (qx *)input_01,
 phi1);
// step 2
qx_matrix_mmul (4,4,1, (qx *)mout0, phi1, phi2);
// step 3
qx_matrix_mmul (4,4,1, (qx *)haid, phi2, phi3);
// step 4
qx_state_measurement(4, phi3, measured);
// retrieve value of x in output state
char x_in_output =
 qx_state_variable_binary_value(4, measured, 0);
```

To initialize ide2 we used a function that accepts as a parameter the base 2 logarithm of the size of the matrix, and which we shall later use also for Hadamard for dimensions greater than 2. The code is:

```
extern BOOL qx_matrix_constant (int casevalue, int
 intpower, qx *dd) // log base 2 of dimension
{
int j, k, dimension;
if ( intpower > 30 ) return FALSE;
  // dimension = 2 pow(intvalue)
  // (32768 for parameter 15)
  dimension = (1 << intpower);
  double divisor;
  switch ( casevalue )
  {
  default: return FALSE;
  case QX_M22_IDEN: // identity of n dimensions
    for ( j = 0; j < dimension; ++j )
    {
      for ( k = 0; k < dimension; ++k )
      {
        dd[(j*dimension)+k].a = ((j == k ) ? 1.0 : 0.0
          );
        dd[(j*dimension)+k].b = 0.0;
      }
    }
  break;
```

```
case QX_M22_HADA:
  // pow N of Hadamard (tensor product)
  double S2I;
  S2I = 1.0/(sqrt(pow(2.0, (double)intpower)));
  for ( j = 0; j < dimension; ++j )
  {
    for ( k = 0; k < dimension; ++k )
    {
      // sign is - if the number of bit == 1
      // in (j & k) is odd
      int test = (j & k);
      int xbit, x, is_parity = 0;
      for ( xbit = 1, x = 0; x < intpower; ++x, xbit
       <<= 1 )
      {
        if ( test & xbit ) is_parity = (1 -
          is_parity);
      }
      dd[(j*dimension)+k].b = 0;
      if ( is_parity ) dd[(j*dimension)+k].a = -S2I;
      else dd[(j*dimension)+k].a = S2I;
    }
  }
  break;
}
return TRUE;
}
```

Notice that what happens to y in the algorithm doesn't interest us. At the end x is measured because it is the action on x that answers the question and gives a solution to the problem.

Now let us check the evolution of the states with constant input $|01\rangle$ and with the four functions, which can be verified with *QcNooq* (points 6.1.D and 6.1.E) or by performing the calculations by hand:

Function	Step	Initial state	0	1	0	0	x in output
	1	after HAHA	1/2	−1/2	1/2	−1/2	
	2	after U$_f$	1/2	−1/2	1/2	−1/2	
0 constant	3	after HAID	$1/\sqrt{2}$	$-1/\sqrt{2}$	0	0	
	4	after Measurement	0	1	0	0	0
		or	1	0	0	0	

Function	Step	Initial state	0	1	0	0	x in output
input	1	after HAHA	1/2	−1/2	1/2	−1/2	
	2	after U$_f$	1/2	−1/2	−1/2	1/2	
	3	after HAID	0	0	1/√2	−1/√2	
	4	after Measurement	0	0	1	0	1
		or	0	0	0	1	

Function	Step	Initial state	0	1	0	0	x in output
NOT input	1	after HAHA	1/2	−1/2	1/2	−1/2	
	2	after U$_f$	−1/2	1/2	1/2	−1/2	
	3	after HAID	0	0	−1/√2	1/√2	
	4	after Measurement	0	0	1	0	1
		or	0	0	0	1	

Function	Step	Initial state	0	1	0	0	x in output
1 constant	1	after HAHA	1/2	−1/2	1/2	−1/2	
	2	after U$_f$	−1/2	1/2	−1/2	1/2	
	3	after HAID	−1/√2	1/√2	0	0	
	4	after Measurement	1	0	0	0	0
		or	0	1	0	0	

For each function, the measurement step has two possibilities, because the state of the system after step 3 always has two values with the same probability of being intercepted by measurement and two values with probability equal to zero. That is, after step 3 we can have:

x	y	
0	0	±1/√2
0	1	±1/√2
1	0	0
1	1	0

which once measured will give x=0 and (y=0 or y=1), that is $|00\rangle$ or $|01\rangle$, or we can have:

x	y	
0	0	0
0	1	0
1	0	$\pm 1/\sqrt{2}$
1	1	$\pm 1/\sqrt{2}$

which once measured will give x=1 and (y=0 or y=1), that is $|10\rangle$ or $|11\rangle$. So in both possibilities, whatever the random value of the measurement, it happens that:

- for the two constant functions x in output is 0
- for the two balanced functions x in output is 1

and therefore it is sufficient to run the circuit of Deutsch's algorithm once to decide whether the function is constant or balanced.

In *QcNooq* 6.1.E you will find the development of the calculations for all four cases of the input. Note that for the input $|00\rangle$ and $|10\rangle$ the algorithm gives no useful result, while for the input $|11\rangle$ the algorithm gives the inverse result to that given for $|01\rangle$, which also would allow us to answer the initial question.

Why does Deutsch answer the problem?

We have not given a rigorous demonstration of the algorithm, but the table of the four cases is sufficient to understand why it gives an answer: after step 3 (action with [Hadamard]$\otimes$[Identity]), for the constant functions there is no probability of having the value $|1\rangle$ for $|x\rangle$ in the measurement, while for the balanced functions there is no probability of having $|0\rangle$ for $|x\rangle$. This conclusion is without exception, and note that it derives entirely from the properties of the operations on the matrices, without any assumptions about the hardware, which is assumed to be capable of processing the input by returning the output corresponding to the operations on the matrices described.

Leaving aside the obvious consideration that all this can have no other use than that of introducing the basic idea of quantum algorithms, I leave it to the reader to reflect on this question, which has probably already appeared obscurely to him: what would happen if the other quantum algorithms were just expansions of this technique?

Usual notation for quantum circuits

There is a standard for the graphic representation of quantum circuits, using which the representation of Deutsch's algorithm:

$$([H]\otimes[I])\ U_f\,([H]\otimes[H])\ |0,1\rangle.$$

would be the following:

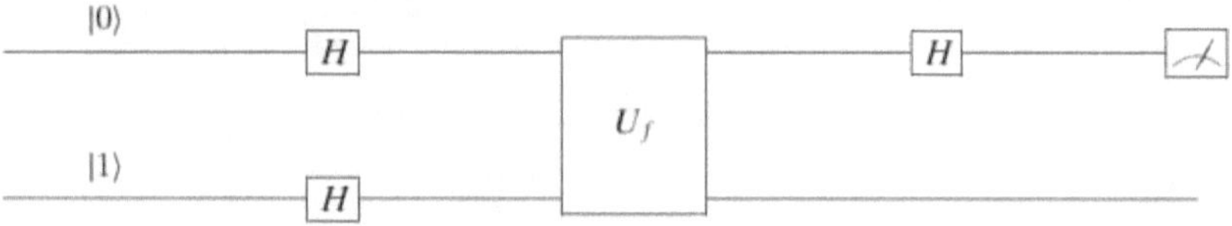

This representation corresponds to the table of steps we used above, and interpretation is very simple:

- the direction of execution of the algorithm in time is from left to right (while the formula representation puts the multipliers used subsequently on the left);
- $|0\rangle$ and $|1\rangle$ represent a qubit, while bold $|0\rangle$ and $|1\rangle$ represent a vector;
- the horizontal lines correspond to a single qubit;
- this representation of a horizontal line:

$$\underline{\qquad /^{n}\qquad}$$

  corresponds to a vector of n qubits;

- and the image of an analog instrument corresponds to the measurement.

Matrices are represented as rectangles, and it is not necessary to represent the identity, where a qubit is unchanged.

6.2 Deutsch–Josza algorithm

In this algorithm, we deal with functions similar to those of the simple Deutsch algorithm, but the input data is a vector of N bits x[N], while the output data is still one bit. So at the input we have a vector of 2, 3, 4 ... bits, and at the output $|0\rangle$ or $|1\rangle$. The basic function has the prototype:

$$\text{bit func(bit input\_vector[]);}$$

and we shall call:

- *constant* any function which, executed for all possible values of x[N], returns $|0\rangle$ in any case or $|1\rangle$ in any case. Hence the constant functions are 2 for any dimension of x[N].

- *balanced* every function that executed for all possible values of x[N], returns the same number of $|0\rangle$ and $|1\rangle$. The number of balanced functions is a function of N (we shall see later which one).

- *neutral* any other function, which returns a number of $|0\rangle$ different from the number of $|1\rangle$. The number of neutral functions will be neutral = total − 2 − balanced.

The Deutsch–Josza algorithm (DJ hereinafter) provides a technique for knowing (ideally) through a single execution which of the three types a function belongs to. For each N, there is a certain number of different functions (we shall see how many shortly) and there is a certain number of possible inputs: with N=2 the possible inputs are 4, and in general they are 2^N. In the case of N=3 the 8 possible inputs are:

x_0	x_1	x_2
0	0	0
0	0	1
0	1	0
0	1	1
1	0	0
1	0	1
1	1	0
1	1	1

Without DJ, with N=3, given any of the many possible functions, we would have to execute the function at least 6 times and in some cases 8 times with different input to know which of the three classes the function belongs to. In fact, suppose we have had 7 times 0: we must execute the function for the eighth time to find out if the function is constant zero (if it returns again 0) or neutral (if it returns 1). Instead, suppose we had: [1111] from 4 executions: the function can still be of any type. Suppose the fifth execution returns 1: we had 5 times 1, and then it could come out 3 times 0 (and then the function would be neutral) or three times 1 (and then the function would be constant). We execute the sixth time: if the return is 0 we can stop, because 1 has gone out 5 times, 0 once and the function is definitely neutral. On the other hand, if after 4 times one we have a zero, we must continue until the end to find out if the function is balanced. In general, we must execute the function for at least half+2 of the cases of the input to assign the function to a class. Instead DJ gives us information on the class to which the function belongs even with a single execution.

The basic functions can be represented with rectangular matrices. With $N = 2$, the function that returns constant zero is:

1	1	1	1
0	0	0	0

Representing the input data as $|\psi\rangle$, with $N = 2$ the input data is a column of 4 elements with 4 possible cases:

$$00 = \begin{bmatrix} 1 \\ 0 \\ 0 \\ 0 \end{bmatrix}$$

$$01 = \begin{bmatrix} 0 \\ 1 \\ 0 \\ 0 \end{bmatrix}$$

$$10 = \begin{bmatrix} 0 \\ 0 \\ 1 \\ 0 \end{bmatrix}$$

$$11 = \begin{bmatrix} 0 \\ 0 \\ 0 \\ 1 \end{bmatrix}$$

and it is immediate that the product of the matrix of the example by each of the 4 cases returns [10], i.e. $|0\rangle$.

Here too, to execute any of the functions inside the DJ algorithm, we must represent each basic function, represented by a non-reversible rectangular matrix, so that the function is executable by a quantum circuit, therefore with a reversible U_f matrix that allows to implement the procedure:

Step: 0	1	2
$\lvert x[N]\rangle$	$[U_f]$	$\lvert x[N]\rangle$
$\lvert y\rangle$		$\lvert y{\wedge}f(x[N])\rangle$

where $\lvert x[N]\rangle$ is the input vector, $\lvert y\rangle$ is one of the two possible values of the function output, and the circuit output repeats $\lvert x[N]\rangle$ unchanged and returns $\lvert f(x[N]){\wedge}y\rangle$, from which we can get $\lvert f(x[N])\rangle$. Remember that $\lvert x[N]\rangle$ is a vector of N bits, but $\lvert f(x[N])\rangle$ is one bit.

Now we want to take these steps:

1. implement a technique with which to construct all possible functions as unitary matrices for a value of N.

2. perform the basic functions represented as unit matrices and verify the output.

3. describe the DJ algorithm.

4. implement the DJ algorithm and verify that with a single action it is able to give us information on the class to which any function belongs.

Let us now construct the matrix U_f first for the case $N = 2$ and then for the case $N = 3$. The case $N = 1$ is that of Deutsch's algorithm discussed above, and it makes no sense to treat it here.

With $N = 2$, we have 16 basic functions, because the 4 possible inputs can give 16 outputs, from 0 constant to 1 constant:

x_0	x_1		f_0	f_1	f_2	f_3	f_4	f_5	f_6	f_7	f_8	f_9	f_{10}	f_{11}	f_{12}	f_{13}	f_{14}	f_{15}
0	**0**		0	0	0	0	0	0	0	0	1	1	1	1	1	1	1	1
0	**1**		0	0	0	0	1	1	1	1	0	0	0	0	1	1	1	1
1	**0**		0	0	1	1	0	0	1	1	0	0	1	1	0	0	1	1
1	**1**		0	1	0	1	0	1	0	1	0	1	0	1	0	1	0	1

Note that in general the possible functions are 2 raised to 2^N: the rows of possible values are 2^N, and the columns of possible functions are consequently 2 raised to 2^N. With $N = 2$ the functions are $2^4 = 16$, with $N = 3$ they are $2^8 = 256$, with $N = 4$ they are $2^{16} = 65536$. Among these, two functions are constant, others for a certain number are balanced, the others are neutral. And precisely, how many balanced functions are there? There are $(2^N)!/((2^{N-1})!)^2$, and therefore with $N = 2$ they are $4!/(2!)^2 = 24/4 = 6$. Verify that in the table there are 6 columns that have twice 1 and twice 0.

Now, let us consider any two bit function, for example the one that returns [0101], which is the function f_5. We have to construct the matrix U_f, which will have a row for each case of $\lvert x[N]\rangle$ and $\lvert y\rangle$, and a column for each case of $|x[N]\rangle$ and $|f(x[N])^\wedge y\rangle$. Therefore, having to represent also the output bit, the square matrix will have dimension 2^{N+1}, in our case $2^3 = 8$. To proceed step by step, we build the 8 possible cases of $|x[N]\rangle$ and $|y\rangle$, we calculate first $f(x[N])$, then $f(x[N])^\wedge y$, and we populate the matrix U_f with the appropriate values (without writing zeros for readability):

| | | | | | | x_0 | 0 | 0 | 0 | 0 | 1 | 1 | 1 | 1 |
| | | | | | | x_1 | 0 | 0 | 1 | 1 | 0 | 0 | 1 | 1 |
x_0	x_1	y	f(x)	f(x)^y	f(x[N])^y	0	1	0	1	0	1	0	1
0	0	0	0	0		1							
0	0	1	0	1			1						
0	1	0	1	1					1				
0	1	1	1	0				1					
1	0	0	0	0						1			
1	0	1	0	1							1		
1	1	0	1	1									1
1	1	1	1	0								1	

In this way we have the U_f function which will allow us to perform the basic function in a quantum algorithm. However, to verify the DJ algorithm with all cases even with only N=2, we shall have to run it 16 times for the 16 basic functions and verify that it can tell us of each function whether it is constant, balanced or neutral. So before proceeding let us see how we can build the 16 U_f matrices with a program. To do this, for each base function, which is a 4-bit vector func_values[4] which gives us the output for the four cases of x_0 and x_1, we need to build a Ufunc[8][8] matrix initialized to zero, then develop the 8 cases of x_0, x_1 and y, calculate f(x) by reading it from func_values[], calculate f(x)^y and assign 1 to Ufunc[][]. The index in func_values[] is the one that corresponds to the current case of x_0 and x_1, therefore x_0*2+x_1. The line in Ufunc[][] is the one that corresponds to the current case of x_0, x_1 and y, so x_0*4+x_1*2+y. The column in Ufunc[][] is the one that corresponds to the current case of x_0, x_1 and f(x)^y, so $x_0*4+x_1*2+f(x)^\wedge y$. The code is as follows:

```
char func_values[4] = {0,1,0,1};
int x0, x1, y, fx, fx_xor_y;
int Urow, Ucol;
qx Ufunc[8][8];
// zero matrix:
memset (Ufunc, 0, 8*8*sizeof(qx));
for (x0 = 0; x0 <= 1; ++x0)
{
  for (x1 = 0; x1 <= 1; ++x1)
```

```
{
  for (y = 0; y <= 1; ++y)
  {
    fx = func_values[x0*2 + x1];
    fx_xor_y = fx^y;
    Urow = x0*4 + x1*2 + y;
    Ucol = x0*4 + x1*2 + fx_xor_y;
    Ufunc[Urow][Ucol].a = 1;
  }
 }
}
```

And with that we built Ufunc for the basis function [0101]. But we
have to do the job 16 times, and if we want to verify everything even
with N = 3 we shall have to do it 256 times. Much better to include
everything in a cycle of the 16 possible functions. To have the 16
cases of the func_values[4] table, we use a very simple trick: the 16
cases range from [0000] to [1111], so they correspond to the binary
representation of the integers between 0 and 15. Therefore to develop
the 16 cases we develop a loop with an index func_idx from 0 to 15
and we obtain the corresponding vector func_values[4] by means of
a function that gives us the binary representation of any integer. In
the *QcNooq* library we have an utility which constructs in destination
the vector corresponding to the binary representation of the number:

```
extern void qx_binary_vector (char *destination,
 int length, unsigned int number)
{
char binary[128+1];
// a 128 bit number can be represented
int bx = 0, mask = 1;
  for (int i = 0; i < length; ++i)
  {
    if((mask&number) >= 1) binary[bx] = 1;
    else binary[bx] = 0;
    ++bx;
    mask<<=1;
  }
  --bx;
  for (; bx >= 0; --bx )
  {
    *dest = binary[bx]; ++dest;
  }
}
```

So the procedure to construct the matrices corresponding to the 16
functions is (*QcNooq* 6.2.A):

```
char func_values[4]; // NOT INITIALIZED
unsigned char func_idx; // index of base function
int x0, x1, y, fx, fx_xor_y;
int Urow, Ucol;
qx Ufunc[8][8];
for (func_idx = 0; func_idx < 16; ++func_idx)
{
  qx_binary_vector(func_values, 4, func_idx);
  memset (Ufunc, 0, 8*8*sizeof(qx));
  for (x0 = 0; x0 <= 1; ++x0)
  {
    for (x1 = 0; x1 <= 1; ++x1)
    {
      for (y = 0; y <= 1; ++y)
      {
        fx = func_values[x0*2 + x1];
        fx_xor_y = fx^y;
        Urow = x0*4 + x1*2 + y;
        Ucol = x0*4 + x1*2 + fx_xor_y;
        Ufunc[Urow][Ucol].a = 1;
      }
    }
  }
  // now the Ufunc matrix corresponding to
  // func_idx is built
  // we can check it or run Deutsch_Josza
  // ACTIONS on Ufunc ...
}
```

Note that all the above will also work for three bits, giving the appropriate dimensions to vectors and matrices. Once this is done, let us move on to the verification, which has the only aim to check that the implementation is correct (we could skip this step). In the loop of the 16 functions, after the construction of each <u>Ufunc</u> we insert the following call (*QcNooq* 6.2.B):

```
void QCF_DJ_N2_verify(qx Ufunc[8][8])
{
qx invector[8]; // input vector: case of x0, x1, y
int inidx;
qx outvector[8];
int x0, x1, y, fx_xor_y, fx;
int cnt0;
cnt0 = 0;
  for (inidx = 0; inidx < 8; ++inidx)
  {
    memset (invector, 0, 8 * sizeof(qx));
```

```
  invector[inidx].a = 1.0;
  qx_matrix_mmul(8,8,1, (qx *)Ufunc, invector,
   outvector);
  x0 = qx_state_variable_binary_value(8, invector,
   0);
  x1 = qx_state_variable_binary_value(8, invector,
   1);
  y = qx_state_variable_binary_value(8, invector,
   2);
  fx_xor_y = qx_state_variable_binary_value(8,
   outvector, 2);
  fx = fx_xor_y ^ y;
  if (fx == 0) ++cnt0;
 }
 // Output of the function type depending on cnt
  ...
}
```

To this verification function we give the <u>Ufunc</u> matrix to be verified as a parameter; within it, for the eight possible values of the state $|x_0,x_1,y\rangle$ we perform the multiplication:

```
qx_matrix_mmul(8,8,1, (qx *)Ufunc, invector,
 outvector);
```

Then we extract from the output vector the value of $f(x)^{\wedge}y$ extracting the bit having index=2 with:

```
fx_xor_y = qx_state_variable_binary_value(8,
 outvector, 2);
```

and then we find fx from $f(x)^{\wedge}y$ executing the XOR. In the loop we count the occurrences of 0 in fx with a counter <u>cnt0</u>. Since the function is executed 8 times, with redundant y, we could represent the result like this:

```
char *typep;
if (cnt0 == 0) typep = "Constant 1";
else if (cnt0 == 8) typep = "Constant 0";
else if (cnt0 == 4) typep = "Balanced";
else typep = "Neutral";
```

Note that we could also execute the function only 4 times, with $y=|0\rangle$ or $y=|1\rangle$ indifferently. We run it 8 times just to verify that all results are as expected.

At this point, let us run the DJ algorithm. Why the algorithm has the form described here and why it gives the output that we shall see, is discussed and demonstrated in the texts that deal with the subject in a complete way. It is not difficult to understand that the reason why DJ works is the same as Deutsch's: the superposition by means of the Hadamard matrix applied appropriately concentrates the probability of finding certain results with respect to others. Anyway, we here limit ourselves to taking the result of the theory as acquired, and therefore we only assume the formula for performing DJ, which is the following circuit, of which we represent the steps from left to right:

Step:	0	1	2	3	4
x[N]	$x=|0[N]\rangle$	$[H]^{\otimes N}$	$[U_f]$	$[H]^{\otimes N}$	$[M]$
y	$y=|1\rangle$	$[H]$		$[I]$	
Output	φ_0	φ_1	φ_2	φ_3	

and which corresponds to the multiplications:

$$([H]^{\otimes N}\otimes[I])\ U_f\,([H]^{\otimes N}\otimes[H])\ |0[N],1\rangle$$

and in the usual graphic representation to:

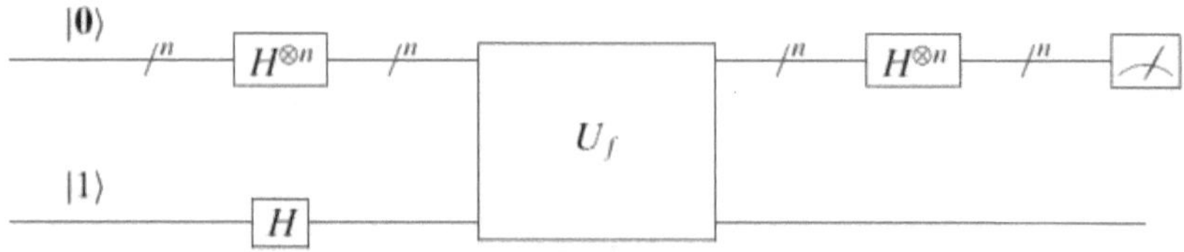

Steps:

0: initialization of the vector $|x[N]\rangle$ with N times zero, initialization of $|y\rangle$ with $|1\rangle$;

1: superposition by acting on everything with Hadamard. The expression $[H]^{\otimes N}$ means that the tensor product is performed N times to create the Hadamard matrix of the necessary dimensions.

2: action with U_f.

3: Hadamard on the output x (and Identity on y).

4: measurement of x.

5: evaluation of the type of function. Here we have an unpleasant surprise: we said earlier that the DJ algorithm *ideally* provides us with information on the type of a basic function with a single U_f execution. The word *ideally* meant that in reality the information provided by DJs is somewhat limited. The measurement, as shown by the circuit, must be performed on the transformed values of x[N] in φ_3 and by running the circuit only once we are granted this knowledge:

- if the bits are both zero, the function is either constant or neutral,

- otherwise the function is either balanced or neutral.

To get a more defined result, we can run the algorithm several times and count the occurrences of 0 and 1 in the two bits of x, to obtain some probable but uncertain information on the class of the function. We have to count the occurrences of zero in the two bits with the counters <u>counter_x00</u> and <u>counter_x10</u> and the total tests with <u>total_counter</u>, and perform the following evaluation:

```
char *type_guessed_p;
if (counter_x00 == total_counter && counter_x10 ==
 total_counter)
  type_guessed_p = "Constant";
else if (counter_x00 == 0 && counter_x10 == 0)
  type_guessed_p = "Balanced";
else if (counter_x00 == total_counter ||
 counter_x10 == total_counter)
  type_guessed_p = "Balanced (or Constant)";
else
  type_guessed_p = "Neutral (or Constant)";
```

That is, after a certain number of samples, if both bits are always equal to zero the probability that the function is constant is very high, if both are always equal to one the probability is for the balanced function, and furthermore we have two other cases where the probability is "balanced, but perhaps constant" and "neutral, but perhaps constant".

The code that runs the circuit without the output statistics is:

```
// constant input from DJ definition
qx x0[2] = {{1},{0}};
qx x1[2] = {{1},{0}};
qx y[2] = {{0},{1}};
qx phix[4];
qx phi0[8], phi1[8], phi2[8], phi3[8], measured[8];
qx HA2[2][2];
qx HA4[4][4];
qx HA8[8][8];
qx ID2[2][2];
qx HA4ID[8][8];
// create phi0 using the tensor product of the
// input constant values
qx_matrix_tensor_product(1,2,1,2, x0, x1, phix);
qx_matrix_tensor_product(1,4,1,2, phix, y, phi0);
// create the constants
qx_matrix_constant(QX_M22_HADA, (qx *)HA2);
qx_matrix_tensor_product(2,2,2,2, (qx *)HA2, (qx
 *)HA2, (qx *)HA4);
qx_matrix_tensor_product(4,4,2,2, (qx *)HA4, (qx
```

```
  *)HA2, (qx *)HA8);
qx_matrix_constant(QX_M22_IDEN, (qx *)ID2);
qx_matrix_tensor_product(4,4,2,2, (qx *)HA4, (qx
 *)ID2, (qx *)HA4ID);
// superposition:
qx_matrix_mmul(8,8,1, (qx *)HA8, phi0, phi1);
// action with Ufunc:
qx_matrix_mmul(8,8,1, (qx *)Ufunc, phi1, phi2);
// superposition on X:
qx_matrix_mmul(8,8,1, (qx *)HA4ID, phi2, phi3);
// measurement:
qx_state_measurement(8, phi3, measured);
```

To create $|\varphi_0\rangle$ we used the tensor product of the input, corresponding to the definition (we could have initialized it for the short ways, knowing that the case is [01000000]). Then we constructed the matrices of the appropriate size for the superposition, acted with the multiplications and finally measured. After measurement we can represent reliable information and probable information with the following code. Note that the counters are vectors, because we need a counter for each of the functions:

```
qx_state_measurement(8, phi3, measured);
outx0 = qx_state_variable_binary_value(8, measured,
 0);
outx1 = qx_state_variable_binary_value(8, measured,
 1);
if (outx0 == 0 && outx1 == 0) type_sure_p =
 "Constant or Neutral";
else type_sure_p = "Balanced or Neutral";
if (outx0 == 0) ++counter_x00[func_idx];
if (outx1 == 0) ++counter_x10[func_idx];
++total_counter[func_idx];
// guessed type after multiple execution
if (counter_x00[func_idx] ==
 total_counter[func_idx] && counter_x10[func_idx]
 == total_counter[func_idx])
type_guessed_p = "Constant";
else if (counter_x00[func_idx] == 0 &&
 counter_x10[func_idx] == 0)
 type_guessed_p = "Balanced";
else if (counter_x00[func_idx] ==
 total_counter[func_idx] || counter_x10[func_idx]
 == total_counter[func_idx])
 type_guessed_p = "Balanced (or Constant)";
else
 type_guessed_p = "Neutral (or Constant)";
```

We evaluated the output to assign a type_sure_p variable with the description of certain information, and then increased and evaluated the counters to assign a type_guessed_p variable with the description of the probable information. In *QcNooq* (6.2.C and 6.2.D) you can find the execution only once and the execution for a very high number of samples (100 times) for all 16 functions.

As in any other case, the purpose of DJ is to find information with a number of cycles lower than that of a classic search. Given any of the functions, the difference with the classical search is that in the classic case after the calculation of a function for only one case we cannot say anything, while with DJ we can say something. After two executions in the classic case only if we have two different results we can exclude that the function is constant, while with DJ we can attribute a probability that is a little richer in information. We shall see in the following algorithms what better can be achieved.

In *QcNooq* (from point 6.2.G onwards) there is the code for DJ with N=3 and 256 functions: you can run it and above all read it to verify that you have fully understood this chapter. You will notice that with N=3 the considerations on the probable class to be attributed change, and that for some functions there is no significant response even after many samplings.

What is the aim of DJ?

The DJ algorithm gives a very approximate answer to the problem posed by exploiting certain properties of the matrices that are used. The most obvious conclusive consideration is that the algorithm is of purely theoretical interest, and that it has no application both for the simplicity of the problem to which it answers, and for the intrinsic limitation of the fact that the answer has a large margin of error. But there is a second consideration that readers who have followed the development should have done by themselves: that the composition of the matrix U_f, indispensable to implement the algorithm, implies the calculation of all the values of the function for the whole range of admissible arguments, and this means that the DJ algorithm is devoid of application for a much more important reason than the approximation of the result: it is devoid of application because the quantum part does not add anything to what is already known during the setup work necessary to execute it. We shall return to this point after having seen the other quantum algorithms.

6.3 Simon's algorithm

Simon's algorithm solves the problem of finding the period (indicated below with the symbol c) of a function that takes as input a bit vector of length N and returns a vector of the same length, and therefore would have the prototype:

$$bit[N] \ func(bit[N]).$$

The period c is defined as a number such that:

$$func(x^{\wedge}c) = func(x).$$

Since $x^{\wedge}0 = x$, for each function there is a period c which is 0. Some functions have a second period other than 0, and precisely they are those having a 2 to 1 relationship between input and output. For example, with N=3 and therefore 3 bits, and therefore x between 0 and 7, if the function were simply:

```
byte base_fx3(byte indata)
{
  return 7-indata;
}
```

we would have a different output for each input, and we would not find a value of c other than 0 that verifies the definition of the period. On the other hand, if the function returned the integer part of the division x/2 and therefore if it were:

```
byte base_fx3(byte indata)
{
  return indata/2;
}
```

we would have the same output for two inputs:

x	0	1	2	3	4	5	6	7
f(x)	0	0	1	1	2	2	3	3

and we would have a period c=1, because, as it is easy to verify, for all these cases we have $func(x) = func(x^{\wedge}1)$:

x	x binary	f(x)	f(x) binary	x^1	x^1 binary	f(x^1)	f(x^1) binary
0	000	**0**	000	1	001	**0**	000
1	001	**0**	000	0	000	**0**	000
2	010	**1**	001	3	011	**1**	001
3	011	**1**	001	2	010	**1**	001
4	100	**2**	010	5	101	**2**	010
5	101	**2**	010	4	100	**2**	010
6	110	**3**	011	7	111	**3**	011
7	111	**3**	011	6	110	**3**	011

The implementation of this algorithm is very compact through the use of the bit operators of the C language, while without them much longer and redundant expressions would be necessary: therefore we shall use C not only to implement the emulation, but also to describe the algorithm. Since we shall describe the algorithm with N=3, remember that every possible value of the 3-bit vector corresponds to a decimal number, and that the powers of 2 correspond to the value of 1 of the bit in the exponent position, so we have:

binary	decimal	power of 2	
000	0		
001	1	2^0	
010	2	2^1	
011	3		=2+1
100	4	2^2	
101	5		=4+1
110	6		=4+2
111	7		=4+2+1

Moreover, we must take into account the properties of bit oriented operations.

Logic operators and bit operators

Reading this note may be omitted by those who know the difference between logic operators and bit operators in C and many programming languages. Otherwise, reading is required to understand the code examples below.

Logic operators convert operands to Boolean values, converting any non-zero value of the operand to 1 (true), and keeping 0 (false) if the operand is zero, and so they always return a Boolean value, 0 or 1. Instead, the bit operators return the result of the logic gate applied to all the bits of the operands, and the type of the result is that of the operands, or of the larger operand of the two. Recall that there are the following operators, with distinct symbols:

6. Quantum Algorithms

Operator	Logic	Bit
NOT	!	~
AND	&&	&
OR	||	|
XOR	not defined	^

So if we suppose we have two bytes a and b, with a=4 and b=5, the logic operators return a bit (Boolean) and we have the following cases:

Operator	Logic operator	Decimal values	Operation executed	Result
NOT	!a	!4	!1	0
	!b	!5	!1	0
AND	a&&b	4&&5	1&&1	1
OR	a||b	4||5	1||1	1

Instead, the bit operators give us a byte and with a=4 and b=5 we have the following cases:

Operator	Bit operator	Binary values	Result
NOT	~a	~00000100	11111011
	~b	~00000101	11111010
AND	a&b	00000100&00000101	00000100
OR	a|b	00000100|00000101	00000101
XOR	a^b	00000100^00000101	00000001

Obviously, when implementing any algorithm we shall be forced to perform bit oriented operations always on multiples of 8 bits (integers of 1, 2, 4 or 8 bytes). Therefore, to be sure to keep only the bits that interest us, after the operations on bits we shall always execute & with a constant chosen so to zero the bits we do not need. For example, in the implementation of Simon's algorithm with N=3 (three bits), after having operated on bits obtaining a byte fx, to be sure to keep only the 3 least significant bits we shall execute:

$$fx = fx\&7 \text{ (i.e., } fx = fx \& [111]).$$

If we were to apply the NOT gate on a=4 and keep only 3 bits, we should execute: fx=(~a)&7 in order to clear the bits out of our range. The operations performed would be:

	Binary values	Result	Decimal result
~4	~00000100	11111011	251 (=128+64+32+16+8+2+1)
(~4)&7	11111011&00000111	00000011	3 (=2+1)

Recall that there are also the left shift a<<X and right shift a>>X operators, which move all the bits of the operand X times, as in this example:

Input	Binary	Operation	Binary result	Decimal result
4	00000100	4<<2	00010000	16
4	00000100	4>>1	00000010	2

Also remember that x<<1 multiplies x by 2 and x>>1 divides x by 2, and consequently the expression (1<<N) is the simplest and most natural way to calculate a power of 2, i.e. is 2^N. For example, $1<<3 = 2^0<<3 = 1000$ binary $= 8 = 2^3$. We shall take advantage of this property in the following implementations.

Let us now come back to Simon's algorithm, with N=3 for simplicity. We must find the period of certain functions, knowing that if each output corresponds to two inputs, then there is also a period c other than zero, otherwise the only solution is c=[000]. The following function, which simply returns a constant according to a correspondence table with the input assuming that the input parameter is in the range [000]–[111], has a period c other than zero:

```
byte base_fx3(byte indata)
{
// ............... in .... { 0, 1, 2, 3, 4, 5, 6, 7 };
static byte output[8] = { 4, 1, 5, 7, 1, 4, 7, 5 };
  return output[indata];
}
```

In fact, the output has the values 4, 1, 5, 7 each repeated twice:

x		f(x)	
0	000	4	100
1	001	1	001
2	010	5	101
3	011	7	111
4	100	1	001
5	101	4	100
6	110	7	111
7	111	5	101

The period of the function (besides 0) is 5, or [101] because:

x		f(x)		x^5		f(x^5)	
0	000	4	100	5	101	4	100
1	001	1	001	4	100	1	001
2	010	5	101	7	111	5	101
3	011	7	111	6	110	7	111
4	100	1	001	1	001	1	001
5	101	4	100	0	000	4	100
6	110	7	111	3	011	7	111
7	111	5	101	2	010	5	101

Obviously the content of the function could be a very complicated calculation, but this is not relevant to Simon's algorithm: therefore we defined the function in the most trivial way possible, and we could also have used simply y=x/2.

To find the period in the slowest, but easiest way, we need to try the possible values of c from 0 to 7 for all possible x, running the following code (*QcNooq* 6.3.B):

```
byte c, x, x_xor_c;
// execution with c = 0 is unnecessary, but
// we include 0 to complete the test
for (c = 0; c < 8; ++c)
{
  for (x = 0; x < 8; ++x)
  {
   // zero not relevant bits
   x_xor_c = (x^c) & 0x07;
   if (base_fx3(x_xor_c) != base_fx3(x)) break;
  }
  if (x == 8) // condition verified
  {
   // display the period c ....
   break; // break cycle on retrieval of c
  }
}
```

For precision sake, with 3 bits, in the worst case we would have to execute the outer loop 6 times, because the execution for c=0 is useless, and if we know that the function is of the type for which there is a $c \neq 0$, after the loop for the value 6 it is not necessary to perform the seventh cycle, because we already know that if c was not yet found we have c=7. There are ways to better optimize the search with classical methods, but we don't care about this.

Instead, we must now resume the notion of the inner product (see section 3.2) and remember, in addition to the general definition, that there is a reduced version of the inner product for bit vectors, which returns a bit, which in the implementation obviously must be represented in a byte, of which only the least significant bit will have meaning. For each value in the range from 0 to $2^N - 1$ (for us from 0 to 7) we can execute $\langle v,c \rangle$ obtaining a bit, that is, we can execute:

```
byte inpr, value;
if (cfound != 0)
{
  for (value = 0; value < 8; ++value)
  {
    inpr = qx_bit_inner_product(3, value, cfound);
    // display inpr = <value,c> ....
  }
}
```

and for the function we have adopted we obtain these values (which can be calculated with *QcNooq* 6.3.B):

value		c		$\langle$value,c$\rangle$
0	000	5	101	0
1	001	5	101	1
2	010	5	101	0
3	011	5	101	1
4	100	5	101	1
5	101	5	101	0
6	110	5	101	1
7	111	5	101	0

Recall that as the general inner product on vectors of real or complex numbers returns a scalar (and not a vector), so the inner product on bit vectors returns a bit, not a bit vector. We shall need the inner product shortly.

To perform the function inside a quantum algorithm, we need to convert it into a unitary matrix U_f that allows us to perform, as always:

Step: 0	1	2
$\|x[N]\rangle$	$[U_f]$	$\|x[N]\rangle$
$\|y[N]\rangle$		$\|y[N]\verb|^|f(x[N])\rangle$

and this time, since we have both an input vector and an output vector, the matrix will have the dimension 2^{2N}, in our case $2^6 = 64$. To build the matrix we can run this code (*QcNooq* 6.3.C):

```
qx Ufunc[64][64];
int j, n_row, n_col;
byte x, y, fx, y_xor_fx;
memset (Ufunc, 0, 64*64*sizeof(qx));
for (j = 0; j < 64; ++j)
```

```
{
  x = (j & (32|16|8)) >> 3;
  y = (j & (4|2|1));
  // this is the classical calculation of f(x):
  fx = base_fx3(x);
  y_xor_fx = y^fx;
  n_row = x*8 + y;  // REDUNDANT: row is j
  n_col = x*8 + y_xor_fx;
  Ufunc[n_row][n_col].a = 1.0;
}
```

The code works like this: we run through the matrix for the 64 rows with j. To determine the values of x corresponding to row j we must take the 3 most significant bits and shift them to the right by 3 positions, while to determine the values of y we must take the 3 least significant bits:

```
x = (j & (32|16|8)) >> 3;
y = (j & (4|2|1));
```

Then we calculate the value of the function with:

```
fx = base_fx3(x);
```

and we determine the column in which we must assign the value 1 to the real part of the complex number with the same method used for DJ in the previous section:

```
y_xor_fx = y^fx;
n_col = x*8 + y_xor_fx;
```

Note that the computation of the row n_row is inserted for clarity, but it is redundant, because n_row corresponds to j. However, we should execute it if we ran through the matrix with two loops, one outside for x and one inside for y.

QcNooq (6.4.D) now allows us to visualize the matrix, verify that it is unitary (it cannot fail to be: but with the verification we make sure that we have not made any mistakes) and try it with random values. Assuming Ufunc was built, we can run:

```
qx invector[64], outvector[64];
int j;
byte x, y, y_xor_fx, fx;
j = qx_random() % 64;
memset (invector, 0, 64 * sizeof(qx));
invector[j].a = 1; // chosen row of matrix
qx_matrix_mmul(64,64,1,(qx *)Ufunc, invector,
  outvector);
x = (qx_state_variable_binary_value(64, invector,
  0)<<2) + (qx_state_variable_binary_value(64,
```

```
invector, 1)<<1) +
 (qx_state_variable_binary_value(64, invector, 2));
y = (qx_state_variable_binary_value(64, invector,
 3)<<2) + (qx_state_variable_binary_value(64,
 invector, 4)<<1) +
 (qx_state_variable_binary_value(64, invector, 5));
y_xor_fx =
(qx_state_variable_binary_value(64,outvector,
 3)<<2) +
 (qx_state_variable_binary_value(64,outvector,
 4)<<1) +
 (qx_state_variable_binary_value(64,outvector, 5));
fx = y_xor_fx ^ y;
// output x,y,fx for verification ...
```

Pay attention to the interpretation of the input and output: after having built <u>invector</u> by choosing a random element and calculated <u>outvector</u> with the usual multiplication, we must extract the bits of x which are the variables 0, 1 and 2 of <u>invector</u> (counting the variables from the right to the left) and the bits of y which are variables 3, 4 and 5. Then for each variable x and y we have to compose a byte with the 3 bits we extracted. For example, with $j = 19$, extracting the three bits of x by from the variables 0, 1 and 2 from <u>invector</u> would give: 0, 1, 0. To compose x as a byte, we execute $(0<<2)+(1<<1)+0$, obtaining $x = 2$ ($=010$ binary). Same for y. With the same technique we extract $y^\wedge f(x)$ from <u>outvector</u>, and then we get $f(x)$. Finally we can represent x and $f(x)$ to verify that the calculation via U_f gives the same results as the calculation with the function base_fx3().

At this point Simon's algorithm joins the game, which readers probably expect to have the aim to find the period c. Actually, it is not able to find the period c, but it is able to give us some elements with fewer iterations than non-quantum search. The circuit is simply this:

Step:	0	1	2	3	4
x[N]	$x=|0[N]\rangle$	$[H]^{\otimes N}$		$[H]^{\otimes N}$	[M]
y[N]	$y=|0[N]\rangle$	[I]	$[U_f]$	[I]	
Output	φ_0	φ_1	φ_2	φ_3	

or:

$$([H]^{\otimes N}\otimes[I])\, U_f\, ([H]^{\otimes N}\otimes[I])\, |0[N],0[N]\rangle$$

and in the usual graphic representation:

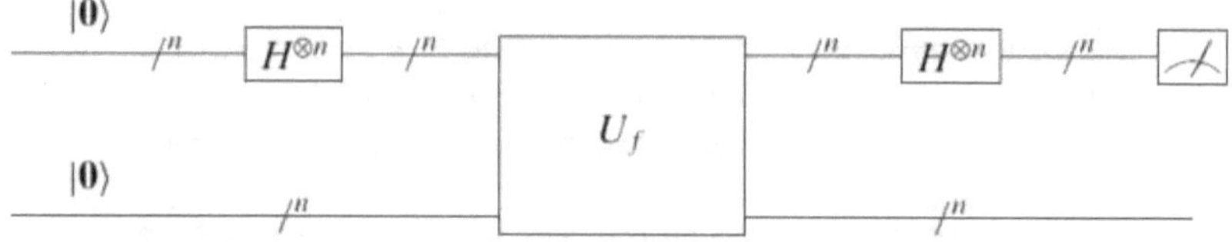

Steps:

0: initialization of input and output to 0 [N].

1: input in superposition with Hadamard of the appropriate size.

2: action with U_f.

3: new superposition on x.

4: measurement of x (y does not matter).

What is the aim this circuit? It is shown that the measurement always returns a vector z such that $\langle z,c \rangle = 0$ ($\langle z,c \rangle$ is the inner product at the bit level). We can implement the circuit and try it a few times with random inputs, and see that the z value always belongs to the set of values for which the inner product with c gives 0. We have seen above that in our example these values are:

value		c		$\langle$value,c$\rangle$
0	000	5	101	0
2	010	5	101	0
5	101	5	101	0
7	111	5	101	0

The code is the following (*QcNooq* 6.3.E):

```
qx phi0[64], phi1[64], phi2[64], phi3[64],
 measured[64];
qx HA8[8][8];
qx ID8[8][8];
qx HA8ID8[64][64];
byte z;
// necessary constants
qx_matrix_constant(QX_M22_HADA, 3, (qx *)HA8);
qx_matrix_constant(QX_M22_IDEN, 3, (qx *)ID8);
qx_matrix_tensor_product(8,8,8,8, (qx *)HA8, (qx
 *)ID8, (qx *)HA8ID8);
// phi0 = [1000.....]
memset (phi0, 0, sizeof(phi0));
phi0[1].a = 1.0;
qx_matrix_mmul(64,64,1, (qx *)HA8ID8, phi0, phi1);
qx_matrix_mmul(64,64,1, (qx *)Ufunc, phi1, phi2);
qx_matrix_mmul(64,64,1, (qx *)HA8ID8, phi2, phi3);
qx_state_measurement(64, phi3, measured);
```

```
z = (qx_state_variable_binary_value(64, measured,
 0)<<2) + (qx_state_variable_binary_value(64,
 measured, 1)<<1) +
 (qx_state_variable_binary_value(64, measured, 2));
//now display z for verification ....
```

Here too we have used the version of qx_matrix_constant() which allows us to give the power of 2 ($\log_2$) of the matrix size as a parameter. For the initialization of phi0 we use the shortest way, since having to initialize everything to zero we know that the element to be set to 1 is the real part of phi0[0]. After having run the multiplications and measured, we extract the values corresponding to the 3 bits of the input, and by running the code more than once we can verify that z belongs to the set of expected values.

At this point, to find c, the circuit must be run a few times, until N values of z have been found, all different among them and different from 0. With N = 3, after having found three values z_A, z_B and z_C, we can set up the following system of equations:

$$\langle z_A,c\rangle = 0;$$
$$\langle z_B,c\rangle = 0;$$
$$\langle z_C,c\rangle = 0;$$

Observe that we have three unknowns, which are the 3 bits of c, c0, c1 and c2, and therefore the system can be expressed as:

$$z_{A0}{}^*c_0 + z_{A1}{}^*c_1 + z_{A2}{}^*c_2 = \text{an even number;}$$
$$z_{B0}{}^*c_0 + z_{B1}{}^*c_1 + z_{B2}{}^*c_2 = \text{an even number;}$$
$$z_{C0}{}^*c_0 + z_{C1}{}^*c_1 + z_{C2}{}^*c_2 = \text{an even number;}$$

That is, the numerical calculation of $z_{A0}{}^*c_0 + z_{A1}{}^*c_1 + z_{A2}{}^*c_2$ would give an integer result, but for the definition of the inner product on bits when this number is even the equation corresponds to $\langle z_A,c\rangle = 0$. Now, since to the right of the equal sign we do not have a real number, but we have the information that the result of the operation on the left is even, the solution of the system would require some appropriate trick (the system is not solvable with substitution or determinant or with the other usual methods). The solution of the system in the simplest way could be an interesting exercise, but to verify the result of Simon's algorithm we just need a slow and inelegant loop on the possible values of c, in which we execute the inner product with the values of nonzero z which we have found. When we find that c matches all the N non-zero values of z which we found, then the current value of c is the period sought.

So, let us proceed like this (*QcNooq* 6.3.F). We create a frequency vector for each possible value of z:

```
int z_frequency[8];
```

and we run the circuit many times. After finding z in the measured vector, we increment the frequency of that value:

```
++z_frequency[z];
```

When we realize that we have found 3 values of z greater than zero, we execute:

```
for (c = 0; c < 8; ++c)
{
  // do not test the zero case of z -
  // you would find c=0
  for (found = 0, z = 1; z < 8; ++z)
  {
    if (z_frequency[z] == 0) continue;
    if (qx_bit_inner_product(3, z, c) == 0)
     ++found;
  }
  if (found == 3)
  {
    // the current value of c is the period.
    // Display ....
  }
 }
}
```

By solving the system with this method, which is the simplest and least refined that can be implemented, one realizes that the algorithm's performance is poor: it takes an average of 6 or 7 tests to find three values of z different from zero.

However, in *QcNooq* we can execute the algorithm also with N=6 (from 6.3.G onwards), defining a base function that has a period c=32 in addition to 0. Consult the source code in the project, in which we could create parametric routines to run the algorithm with variable value of N, but we preferred not to do it to maintain better readability.

With N=6, we have:

$$0 \leq x \leq 64$$

and the same for y and for the period c. The vectors $|\varphi\rangle$ take the dimension 64^2, hence 4096, and the matrices for U_f and for the constant operators take the dimension 4096^2, hence 16,777,216. These dimensions are not in bytes, but must be multiplied by the size of the qx structure (16 bytes), and therefore the memory allocation is gigantic.

As for emulation, if we wanted to emulate quantum algorithms with more extensive data, it would become necessary to implement some optimizations, among which:

1. it is not necessary to represent the square matrices U_f with matrices allocated in memory: in each of them for each row there is a single column with the value 1.0, and therefore to represent an U_f it would be enough to use an integer vector in which each element k contains the non-zero column corresponding to row k. Then we should implement the multiplication of a matrix represented in this way by a vector $|\varphi\rangle$.

2. it is not necessary to allocate in memory the matrices corresponding to the constants composed by means of the base gates: it is enough to implement functions that perform the multiplication of the constant of the case by a $|\varphi\rangle$, looking for the row and column values in the cycle that performs the multiplication.

But this would only concern emulation: if a reliable quantum computer working with a useful number of qubits were actually available, the problem of the immense amount of memory of the classical computer that acts as a client of the quantum one, to which certain calculations are delegated, persists and is of great relevance.

By running the algorithm for a 6-bit function, we can notice several things. First of all, that execution is somewhat slow, and it cannot be otherwise. But remember that if the quantum processor were really available, the heart of the operation, that is, the multiplications:

```
qx_matrix_mmul((64*64),(64*64),1,(qx
 *)HA64ID64,phi0,phi1);
qx_matrix_mmul((64*64),(64*64),1,(qx
 *)Ufunc_64,phi1,phi2);
qx_matrix_mmul((64*64),(64*64),1,(qx
 *)HA64ID64,phi2,phi3);
```

would be performed with only three actions, or only three cycles, of the quantum processor, while we have to go through the 4096 rows and columns of the matrices in emulation. Then, we realize that a few cycles, 6 or 7, are enough to find 6 different values of z, because the possible values of z are many and it is unlikely to find the same twice with a few executions of the algorithm. However, sometimes the value of z reveals for the period c, in addition to the correct value, also two other erroneous values, so that with 6 bits it is not certain, but it is only probable, that $\langle z,c\rangle=0$ and that Simon's algorithm can find the period c. This is a limitation that reminds us of that of DJ, which only gives us probable indications on the type of function to which it applies.

What is Simon's algorithm aim?

Just like DJ, Simon's algorithm gives a very approximate answer to the problem posed by exploiting certain properties of the matrices that are used. Given the properties of the Hadamard matrix, it is shown that the measurement always returns a vector z such that $\langle z,c \rangle = 0$, and this property allows us to go back to the period c.

But here too, as we observed for DJ, the composition of the matrix U_f, indispensable to implement the algorithm, implies the calculation of all the values of the basic function for the whole range of admissible arguments, with which the algorithm turns out to be absolutely devoid of any use, even when quantum hardware existed, because the work of compiling the U_f matrix (which the quantum hardware assumes as external data) is in itself demanding as much or more resources than the search for the period through the execution of a classical loop. The reader will now probably assume that more complex algorithms are not subject to this limitation.

6.4 Grover's algorithm

Grover's algorithm is generally referred to as "Grover's search algorithm": but it is appropriate to make soon clear that the algorithm cannot be used for any search in a set of data, and the problem to which it responds has only a certain similarity with the search problem in a database. This preliminary clarification anticipates a conclusion to which it would be right to arrive only after studying the algorithm, however it is appropriate, because in the absence of it readers, while working to understand the algorithm, tend to ask themselves: "but of which kind of research are we talking about?", and this doubt prevents them from quickly focusing on the structure of the algorithm.

The problem is this: suppose we have a function:

bit func(bit vector[N])

which in input has a vector of bits (for example a vector of 3 bits), in output returns 1 for a single value of the vector, such as [101], and returns 0 in any other case. If we want to know for which argument the function returns 1, we must execute the function for [000], [001], etc., and in the worst case we must execute it N times (or N–1 times if we are guaranteed that there is a solution: because in such case if the penultimate argument [110] does not verify the function, we know that the last possible argument [111] must be the solution). If we have many functions with random distribution, on average we have to execute the function N/2 times (or a little less if we know the set of values existing in the vector), because this is the probability of finding the value sought.

This problem has a similarity with the search of an element in an unordered list. In fact, suppose we need to look for a character in a disordered vector like [HGEFCBAD]. If we search for 'D', we have to go through the 8 elements to find it, but if we are sure that each of the 8 letters ABCDEFGH has an occurrence, then we can stop at the penultimate case and deduce that the next one is D. If we have many cases, on average we have to execute N/2 searches for each case, or (N–1)/2 searches if we know that we can apply the rule of not passing the penultimate search in the worst case, because we know that the character we are looking for exists in the array.

Let us now work on 3 bits, and define a trivial function that returns 1 for argument [101], or for argument 5 if we look at the input as a binary expression of a number:

```
byte grover_3bit_base_function(byte input)
```

```
{
  if (input == 5) return 1; // 5 = binary 101
  else return 0;
}
```

The function is in *QcNooq* 6.4.A.

Now we must as always express the function so that we can use it with quantum methods, and therefore so that we can perform:

Step: 0	1	2
$\lvert x[N]\rangle$		$\lvert x[N]\rangle$
$\lvert y\rangle$	$[U_f]$	$\lvert y{\wedge}f(x[N])\rangle$

where $\lvert x[N]\rangle$ is the input vector, $\lvert y\rangle$ is one of the two possible values of the function output, and the circuit output repeats $\lvert x[N]\rangle$ and returns $\lvert f(x[N]){\wedge}y\rangle$, from which we can get $\lvert f(x[N])\rangle$. Remember that $\lvert x[N]\rangle$ is a vector òf N bits, but $\lvert f(x[N])\rangle$ is just one bit. The code that creates and verifies the matrix (*QcNooq* 6.4.B) as always resets the matrix, then for each row it assigns the value 1 to the column corresponding to y^f(x). This is the content of a function that constructs the matrix:

```
void QCF_Buid_Grover_3bit_func_Uf()
{
qx Ufunc[16][16];
byte x, y, fx, y_xor_fx;
int row, col;
qx phi0[16], phi1[16];
  memset(Ufunc, 0, sizeof(Ufunc));
  for (x = 0; x < 8; ++x)
  {
    for (y = 0; y <= 1; ++y)
    {
      fx = grover_3bit_base_function(x);
      y_xor_fx = y^fx;
      row = x * 2 + y;
      col = x * 2 + y_xor_fx;
      Ufunc[row][col].a = 1;
    }
  }
  // output Ufunc for verification ....
}
```

For verification, 1 is assigned to the element of <u>phi0</u> corresponding to each possible value of x, multiplication is performed and the output status is extracted:

```
for (x = 0; x < 8; ++x)
{
```

```
y = 0; // could be 1, it does not matter
memset (phi0, 0, sizeof(phi0));
// input data, row corresponding to x
phi0[x*2+y].a = 1.0;
qx_matrix_mmul(16,16,1, (qx *)Ufunc, phi0, phi1);
// Notice that the binary variable to be
// extracted is 3, i.e. the fourth bit
y_xor_fx =
  qx_state_variable_binary_value(16,phi1,3);
fx = y^y_xor_fx;
// output x and fx ....
}
```

Recall that we have three input bits and one output, so to know f(x) we need to extract the fourth bit from phi1 (variable with index=3):

```
y_xor_fx =
 qx_state_variable_binary_value(16,phi1,3);
```

At this point, Grover's algorithm intervenes with a method that allows us to find the input with which the function returns 1 by executing not N or N–1 cycles, but a smaller number, which we shall initially assign to 3, and then we shall discuss better. To run Grover, we must initialize a matrix of size N (which we call M_IDE_2A) which performs an operation called *inversion around the mean* or *inversion around the average* and is constructed with this rule:

- for $x = y$, $M\_IDE\_2A[x][y] = -1+2/2^N$

- for $x \neq y$, $M\_IDE\_2A[x][y] = 2/2^N$

The code that constructs the matrix is this (*QcNooq* 6.4.C):

```
void QCF_Buid_Grover_average_inversion_matrix(int
 size, qx *MI2A)
{
int r, c;
  for (r = 0; r < size; ++r)
  {
    for (c = 0; c < size; ++c)
    {
     // Take care of floating point. Do not
     // calculate an integer division:
     if (r == c) MI2A[r*size+c].a = -1.0 +
       (2.0/(double)size);
     else MI2A[r*size+c].a = (2.0/(double)size);
     MI2A[r*size+c].b = 0;
    }
  }
}
```

To understand the role this matrix plays, let us use an example that is not part of quantum computation. Suppose we have a vector of N numbers, with N=4, for example: v[4] = {22, 37, 5, 12}. The mean is (22+37+5+12)/4=19. Then we construct a square matrix in which each element [x][y] is equal to 1/N. Multiplying this matrix by the vector we would get a vector in which each element is equal to the mean:

1/4	1/4	1/4	1/4		22					
1/4	1/4	1/4	1/4	*	37	=	19	19	19	19
1/4	1/4	1/4	1/4		5					
1/4	1/4	1/4	1/4		12					

This matrix is not unitary, and could not be used in quantum computation. But let us now define the operation that we called inversion around the mean in this way: each element v[x] of the vector is replaced by:

$$v\_t[x] = mean+(mean-v[x]).$$

So in our example we would have:

v[x]	22	37	5	12
mean+(mean–v[x])	19+(19–22)	19+(19–37)	19+(19–5)	19+(19–12)
v_t[x]	16	1	33	26

The transformed vector is symmetrically arranged above and below the mean line, like this:

v_t:			33	
v_t:				26
mean		19		
v_t:	16			
v_t:		1		

These operations can be verified in *QcNooq* 6.4.D (but it is advisable to check the calculation by hand).

With these premises we can proceed to describe Grover's algorithm. First of all, the M_IDE_2A matrix constructed using the criterion defined above transforms a vector by performing exactly the inversion around the mean operation described above: v[4] becomes v_t[4] as in the example. In the cases that interest us, that is those in which the number of elements of the matrix is a power of 2, the matrix M_IDE_2A is unitary, even if at first sight it does not seem so. In fact, it is shown that if all the elements of a square matrix M are the inverse of a power of 2, then M*M=M, and on the basis of this it can be shown that the inversion matrix around the mean is also unitary. In *QcNooq* we can verify this with qx_matrix_is_unitary(), which obviously has no general demonstration value, but assures us that we are not making mistakes in the implementation.

In our case, for any dimension N of the vector to which U_f is applied, the dimension of U_f is 2^{N+1}, the dimension of M_IDE_2A is 2^N, and therefore M_IDE_2A is unitary. Proceeding with input of N=3 bits, therefore with $U_f[16][16]$, we shall construct M_IDE_2A[8][8].

Then we shall perform the following algorithm procedure, in which a classically controlled cycle executes N_ITERATIONS times the following circuit, with N_ITERATIONS = 3:

Step:	0	1	loop	2	3	4		5
x[N]	x=|0[N]⟩	$[H]^{\otimes N}$	N_ITERATIONS times {	[I]	$[U_f]$	[M_IDE_2A]		[M]
y	y=|1⟩	[I]		[H]		[I]		
Output	φ_0	φ_1		φ_2 / φ_3		φ_4	}	

or:

$$[([M\_IDE\_2A]\otimes[I])U_f([I]^{\otimes N}\otimes[H])]\ ([H]^{\otimes N}\otimes[I])\ |0[N],1\rangle$$

and in the usual graphic representation:

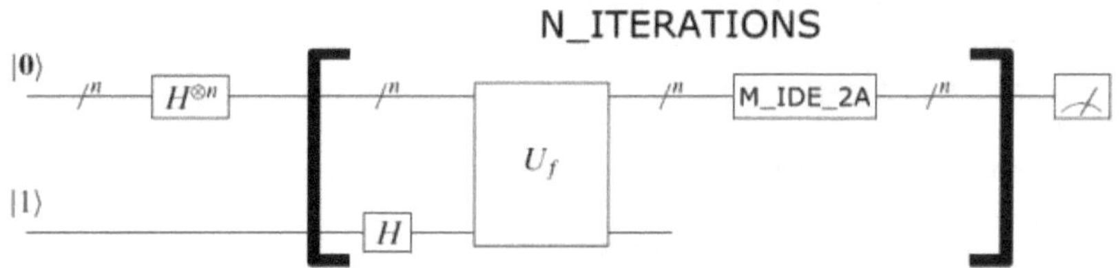

Steps:

0: initialization of x with $|0[N]\rangle$ and y with $|1\rangle$.

1: $|x\rangle$ in superposition with $[H]^{\otimes N}$.

Repetition for N_ITERATIONS:

2: $|y\rangle$ in superposition with [H]

3: action with function U_f.

4: action with the inversion around the mean matrix.

5: measurement of $|x\rangle$.

The algorithm code for three bits is as follows (*QcNooq* 6.4.E), and calls the two functions we have seen above to initialize the U_f matrix and the inversion matrix M_IDE_2A:

```
// Build the acting matrices: Ufunc and inversion
qx Ufunc[16][16];
```

```
QCF_Build_Grover_3bit_func_Uf(Ufunc);
qx M_IDE_2A[8][8];
QCF_Build_Grover_3bit_average_inversion_matrix(8,
 (qx *)M_IDE_2A);
// Build the constant matrices needed:
qx HA[2][2];
qx HA3[8][8];
qx HA4[16][16];
qx IDE1[2][2];
qx IDE3[8][8];
qx IDE3HA[16][16];
qx HA3IDE[16][16];
qx M_IDE_2A_IDE[16][16];
qx_matrix_constant(QX_M22_HADA, (qx *)HA);
qx_matrix_constant(QX_M22_HADA,4,(qx *)HA4);
qx_matrix_constant(QX_M22_HADA,3,(qx *)HA3);
qx_matrix_constant(QX_M22_IDEN, (qx *)IDE1);
qx_matrix_constant(QX_M22_IDEN,3,(qx *)IDE3);
qx_matrix_tensor_product(8,8,2,2,(qx *)M_IDE_2A,(qx
 *)IDE1, (qx *)M_IDE_2A_IDE);
qx_matrix_tensor_product(8,8,2,2,(qx *)IDE3,(qx
 *)HA, (qx *)IDE3HA);
qx_matrix_tensor_product(8,8,2,2,(qx *)HA3,(qx
 *)IDE1, (qx *)HA3IDE);
// now execute Grover
int iteration;
byte xout;
qx phi0[16], phi1[16], phi2[16], phi3[16],
 phi4[16], measured[16];
memset(phi0, 0, sizeof(phi0));
// ww must initialize phi0 with x[3] = 0, y = 1, so
// the significant element is:
phi0[1].a = 1.0;
// first step:
// before the iterazions put |x) in superposition
qx_matrix_mmul(16,16,1,(qx *)HA3IDE, phi0, phi1);
// iterations
#define ITERATIONS_3BIT 3
for (iteration = 0; iteration < ITERATIONS_3BIT;
 ++iteration)
{
 // at every iteration put |y) in superposition
 qx_matrix_mmul(16,16,1, (qx *)IDE3HA, phi1,
  phi2);
 // action with Ufunc
 qx_matrix_mmul(16,16,1, (qx *)Ufunc, phi2, phi3);
```

```
// inversion around the mean
qx_matrix_mmul(16,16,1, (qx *)M_IDE_2A_IDE, phi3,
 phi4);
// output phi4 for verification ....
// assign phil for next iteration
// in the real quantum processor we would have a
// unique vector
// no assigment can occur inside a quantum
// processor
 memcpy (phil, phi4, sizeof(phil));
}
// measurement of phi4
qx_state_measurement(16, phi4, measured);
// extraction of 3 bits of |x) in output
xout =
 (qx_state_variable_binary_value(16,measured,0)<<2)
 +
 (qx_state_variable_binary_value(16,measured,1)<<1)
 +
 (qx_state_variable_binary_value(16,measured,2)<<0)
 ;
// output result of measurement for verification
 ....
}
```

Ufunc is initialized with the usual technique, M_IDE_2A with the above procedure and all the necessary constant matrices are also initialized. Given the input $x=|0\rangle$ and $y=|1\rangle$, in phi0 it is enough to assign value 1 to the second element. The iterations are performed, and remember that if we had a quantum processor, the input vector would be modified, and we would not have the objects phi0, phi1 etc., but the successive states $\varphi0$, $\varphi1$, $\varphi3$, and $\varphi4$ of the same single vector of the physical qubits. Copying phi4 onto phi0 would make no sense inside quantum hardware, where it would not be executable because it is not a reversible operation. Finally, the measurement is performed and the value of transformed x is taken. This has a certain probability of matching the value of x that gives $f(x)=1$, i.e. the value sought.

Now, this is the definition of the algorithm, but why does the algorithm give a result? It gives a result because the effect of Hadamard's action on $|y\rangle$ and of M_IDE_2A on $|x\rangle$ repeated for some iterations is to concentrate the probability in the columns where x corresponds to the value of $f(x)=1$, and to assign a much smaller probability to the other columns. For this reason, the measurement of

$|x\rangle$ then has a high probability of finding the value of x giving f(x)=1. With 3 bits and x=$|101\rangle$, that is 5, the values of x corresponding to f(x)=1 are found in columns 5*2 and 5*2+1, i.e. 10 and 11 (remember that there are two columns: one for y=0, the other for y=1). The action with the matrix that performs the inversion around the mean raises the probability for the columns corresponding to f(x)=1, and the reason why this happens is the subject of a demonstration found in the more formal treatment of the algorithm. It is enough for us to have grasped the underlying idea and understood the rule to execute the algorithm, and to note that in the example with 3 bits and input=$|101\rangle$ we have the following values:

Columns:	0 to 9	10:x=5,f(x)=1,y=0	11:x=5,f(x)=1,y=1	12 to 15
φ_4 after 1 iteration	±0.125	0.625	−0.625	±0.125
φ_4 after 2 iterations	±0.132583	−0.662913	0.309359	±0.132583
φ_4 after 3 iterations	±0.015625	0.953125	0.296875	±0.015625

The sign has no relevance, because we know that probabilities are squared in the measurement. With these values, by performing the measurement after 3 iterations, we have a high probability of detecting xout=5. Now, by executing the function only once (*QcNooq* 6.4.E), it may happen to have xout=5, or not. Executing it a certain number of times (*QcNooq* 6.4.F), we shall see that the probability of reading the value 5 is about 0.997.

And this is Grover's algorithm, which, in this example, finds the value 5 with only 3 iterations of the search instead of the 7 or 8 (or 4 in the average) that could be necessary when proceeding in sequence. That the algorithm is of purely theoretical interest is evident if we think that to create the matrix U_f we must have travelled through all the values of the basic function, and therefore we know everything about it: if the values were many, by following it we could compile an index which would allow to perform the binary search for any input, and it would never be convenient to consult the list with Grover's method. Note that the need to compile an indexed results table instead of repeating the function may occur in reality: for example, the problem of the optimal route for a travelling salesman is known to require very complex and laborious calculations. Our function, instead of being defined in a trivial way and returning a constant as happens in our example, if the problem were that of the travelling salesman could be the answer to the question: "from which destination should I start the journey?", and in such case to keep a solution database would be cheaper than repeating the calculation. Only, Grover's algorithm would have nothing to offer compared to the usual indexing techniques, even if quantum hardware existed to perform multiplications.

There is also a second reason why Grover's algorithm is of purely theoretical interest, and it is that increasing the number of bits does not increase the number of iterations that should be performed (as might be expected), but drastically decreases the probability of finding the correct value. With values from 3 to 7 bits the optimal number of iterations is always 3. With *QcNooq* (from 6.4.A' onwards) you can try to execute the algorithm with number of bits from 4 to 7, and you can change the number of iterations. Observing phi4, it is noted, for example, that the minimum probability value for incorrect values occurs with the third iteration, and then there is another low value with the eleventh iteration. Simply increasing the iterations is not enough to improve probability. For example, with 3 bits the fourth and fifth interaction are disadvantageous, because we have:

3 BIT	Columns 0 to 9	Column 10: x=5,f(x)=1,y=0	Column 11: x=5,f(x)=1,y=1	Columns 12 to 15
φ_4 after1 iteration	±0.125	0.625	−0.625	±0.125
φ_4 after 2 iterations	±0.132583	−0.662913	0.309359	±0.132583
φ_4 after 3 iterations	±0.015625	0.953125	0.296875	±0.015625
φ_4 after 4 iterations	0.11 or 0.23	0.348029	−0.624243	0.11 or 0.23
φ_4 after 5 iterations	±0.236328	−0.348029	−0.624243	±0.236328

As you can see, at the fifth iteration the probability of incorrect values rises from 0.0156 to 0.237, and the repeated execution of the algorithm lowers the frequency of the correct value from 0.997 to about 0.22. With four iterations the frequency of the corrected value is about 0.51.

By increasing the bits and we have the following situation:

4..7 BIT	Columns < f(x)=1	f(x)=1, y=0	f(x)=1,y=1	Columns >f(x)=1
4 bit after 3 iteration	±0.070434	0.921172	0.0511	±0.070434
5 bit after 3 iterations	±0.082886	0.756714	0.037964	±0.082886
6 bit after 3 iterations	±0.072668	0.575722	0.05644	±0.072668
7 bit after 3 iterations	±0.056792	0.422088	−0.050994	±0.056792

At first glance it could be said that the probability of values other than x giving f(x)=1 is always small, and that of the columns for the searched values is prevalent. This is true, but the problem is that the total columns are $2*2^N$, and therefore with 7 bits we have 256 columns, of which 254 contain probabilities of values other than x giving f(x)=1. The result is that by running the algorithm many times with 3 iterations, we have the following frequencies of the correct value of x:

3..7 BIT	Frequency of x giving f(x)=1 with 1000 samples
3 bit after 3 iterations	0.997
4 bit after 3 iterations	0.849
5 bit after 3 iterations	0.57
6 bit after 3 iterations	0.33
7 bit after 3 iterations	0.18

and this would be the output of the quantum hardware, because the quantum hardware is not designed to notice that the frequencies of the two columns searched are greater, but only to extract a result according to the overall probability.

Some more statistics

At this point we might ask: how to find the optimal value of the number of iterations? The maximum number of iterations must be less than 2^N, otherwise Grover's algorithm would have not even a theoretical advantage over sequential search. We could look for this optimal number of iterations purely in a mathematical way by studying the properties of the inversion around the mean, or we could look for it by trying to develop phi4 with all possible values less than 2^N, and looking for the number of iterations for which maximum the overall probability of the two columns corresponding to f(x)=1. To do this, we need to normalize the phi4 vector created by running the algorithm once. The code (*QcNooq* 6.4.G) calls a function to execute Grover with N bits, to which the vector on which to build phi4 is passed as a parameter in order to analyze it in the calling function. The function executing Grover is this (the utilities to build U_f and the inversion matrix are obviously similar to those for 3 bits):

```c
void QCF_Grover_Nbit_algorithm(char verbose, int
 num_samples, qx *phi4)
{
char buf[200];
static int total_ok=0, total_ko=0, total;
#define GROVER_N_BIT_VALUE
 (((1<<number_of_bits)/2)+1)
 if ( num_samples < 0 )
 {
   total_ok = total_ko = total = 0; return;
 }
 QCF_Build_Grover_Nbit_func_Uf((qx *)Ufunc_big);
 QCF_Build_Grover_Nbit_average_inversion_matrix((1
  <<number_of_bits), (qx *)M_IDE_2A_big);
 qx HA[2][2];
 qx IDE1[2][2];
 // cannot be in stack:
 static qx HA3[128][128];
 static qx HA4[256][256];
 static qx IDE3[128][128];
 static qx IDE3HA[256][256];
 static qx HA3IDE[256][256];
 static qx M_IDE_2A_IDE[256][256];
 qx_matrix_constant(QX_M22_HADA, (qx *)HA);
 qx_matrix_constant(QX_M22_HADA,1+number_of_bits,(
  qx *)HA4);
 qx_matrix_constant(QX_M22_HADA,number_of_bits,(qx
  *)HA3);
 qx_matrix_constant(QX_M22_IDEN, (qx *)IDE1);
 qx_matrix_constant(QX_M22_IDEN,number_of_bits,(qx
  *)IDE3);
 qx_matrix_tensor_product((1<<number_of_bits),(1<<
  number_of_bits),2,2,(qx *)M_IDE_2A_big,(qx
  *)IDE1, (qx *)M_IDE_2A_IDE);
 qx_matrix_tensor_product((1<<number_of_bits),(1<<
  number_of_bits),2,2,(qx *)IDE3,(qx *)HA, (qx
  *)IDE3HA);
 qx_matrix_tensor_product((1<<number_of_bits),(1<<
  number_of_bits),2,2,(qx *)HA3,(qx *)IDE1, (qx
  *)HA3IDE);
 int iteration, g;
 byte xout;
 qx phi0[256], phi1[256], phi2[256], phi3[256],
  measured[256];
 // value to be found:
 byte classical_fx = GROVER_N_BIT_VALUE;
```

```c
int sample, local_cnt = 0;
for ( sample = 0; sample < num_samples; ++sample
 )
{
 memset( phi0, 0, sizeof(phi0) );
 // ww must initialize phi0 with x[3] = 0, y = 1,
 // so the significant element is:
 phi0[1].a = 1.0;
 // first step:
 qx_matrix_mmul(2*(1<<number_of_bits),2*(1<<numbe
  r_of_bits),1,(qx *)HA3IDE, phi0, phi1);
 // iterations
 // you can verify what happens with more
 // iteration giving a value != 0 here:
 int optimal_iterations;
 if ( number_of_iterations <= 0 )
 {
 switch ( (1<<number_of_bits) )
 {
  default : optimal_iterations = 0;
  // output "Unknown optimal iteration number";
  return;
  case 4: optimal_iterations = 3; break;
  case 8: optimal_iterations = 3; break;
  case 16: optimal_iterations = 3; break;
  case 32: optimal_iterations = 3; break;
  case 64: optimal_iterations = 3; break;
  case 128: optimal_iterations = 3; break;
  }
 }
 else optimal_iterations = number_of_iterations;
 for ( iteration = 0; iteration <
  optimal_iterations; ++iteration )
 {
  qx_matrix_mmul(2*(1<<number_of_bits),2*(1<<numb
   er_of_bits),1, (qx *)IDE3HA, phi1, phi2);
  qx_matrix_mmul(2*(1<<number_of_bits),2*(1<<numb
   er_of_bits),1, (qx *)Ufunc_big, phi2, phi3);
  qx_matrix_mmul(2*(1<<number_of_bits),2*(1<<numb
   er_of_bits),1, (qx *)M_IDE_2A_IDE, phi3,
   phi4);
  // assign phi1 for next iteration
  memcpy ( phi1, phi4, sizeof(phi1) );
 }
 qx_state_measurement(2*(1<<number_of_bits),
  phi4, measured);
```

```
  for ( xout = 0, g = 0; g < number_of_bits; ++g )
  {
    xout +=
      (qx_state_variable_binary_value(2*(1<<number_o
      f_bits),measured,g)<<((number_of_bits-1)-g));
  }
  if ( xout == classical_fx ) ++total_ok;
  else ++total_ko;
  ++total;
 }
  // the calling function should now analyze phi4
}
```

The code to find the optimal value of the iterations is the following. Recall, reading the code, that (1<<number_of_bits) is the most natural way to calculate 2^N (whoever used the double pow() call to calculate a power of 2 would still be very far from the mindset needed for quantum computing):

```
int nn;
qx phi4[256];
qx phinormal[256];
int best_case_iterations;
int col_fx;
double msq;
qx inverse_length, px;
double best_case;
// this and the next are the colums corresponding
// to fx:
col_fx = 2* GROVER_N_BIT_VALUE;
best_case = best_case_iterations = 0;
for (nn = 3; nn < (1<<number_of_bits); ++nn)
{
  // global value read by call of Grover:
  number_of_iterations = nn;
  // once to have phi4
  // now normalize phi
  QCF_Grover_Nbit_algorithm(0,1, phi4); msq =
   qx_vector_moduli_squared_sum(2*(1<<number_of_bit
   s), phi4);
  inverse_length.a = 1/sqrt(msq); inverse_length.b
   = 0;
  qx_vector_smul(2*(1<<number_of_bits),
   inverse_length, phi4, phinormal);
  // probability to get fx = sum of squares of the
  // values of the two fx columns:
  px = qx_add(qx_mul(phi4[col_fx],phi4[col_fx]),
   qx_mul(phi4[col_fx+1],phi4[col_fx+1]));
  if (px.a > best_case)
```

```
{
  best_case = px.a; best_case_iterations = nn;
  }
}
// best_case_iterations found: display ....
```

Running this algorithm shows us that with 3, 4 and 5 bits the optimal value is 3 executions, with 6 bits it is 11, which can be an advantage since the values to be tested with the sequential search are $2^6 = 64$, and with 7 bits it is 121, very little advantageous with respect to the $2^7 = 128$ possible values, and in any case such that it slightly improves the result obtained with 3 iterations.

Could Grover's algorithm be used to build a database?

The answer is obvious: no. And the reason does not lie either in the complexity of the algorithm or in the approximation of the result, but in the fact that a database in which one wanted to perform a search with this algorithm should be entirely represented not only in the form of a U_f matrix, but in a U_f matrix built ad hoc for each search.

It is well known by all those who know the programming technique that the simplest way to consult an unsorted set of data is to associate an ordered list of search keys. The technique is the ancient one of file cabinets: suppose we have a million folders containing data of as many people, or a million books in a library. In order to search quickly for folders or books by author, we need to compile a million cards indicating the shelf where the book is located, and sort them by surname. Then, when looking for the book, suppose by the author Jones, we shall start from the card that is in the centre of the file, and we shall find an author starting with M. Then we shall neglect all the cards following M (so we shall have halved the cards in which search) and we shall go to the card that is halfway between A and M: we shall find an author starting with D. Now we shall divide the interval between D and M in half (the cards in which to search are now reduced to a quarter of total), and proceeding in this way, always halving the range of cards in which may be the data we are looking for, we shall arrive at the Jones card having performed the operation at most 20 times. This is the binary search technique: if the list has N elements, since at each division the elements to search for are divided in half, the binary search in the ordered list requires a number of readings at most equal to logarithm base 2 of N, after which only one element remains, which is the one sought. So, for example, for a database containing one million elements, since $2^{20}=1.048.576$, the ordered list associated with it allows us to find an element with a maximum of twenty readings, while if for each search we had to go through the set of unsorted data, on average, we would have to perform half a million readings, and in the worst case one million.

Now, arguing that Grover's algorithm is comparable to a search technique is in itself a metaphor, but the literature on quantum algorithms makes a more challenging statement: it argues that Grover's algorithm is capable of performing a search in an unordered set of data without the need to go through it, and this, more than a metaphor, is a fairy tale dictated by illusion. Grover's algorithm finds the data with the inversion around the mean technique because the data are entirely represented in the U_f matrix: but data, whatever their origin, which may be natural (for example, experimental samplings of a phenomenon) or anthropic and cultural (for example, the pupils of schools in a given country) are not met in the form of unitary and invertible matrices useful for quantum algorithms: data are met in the most varied forms of experience, and if we want to represent them in the U_f matrices, it is necessary to go through them entirely and construct the corresponding matrices. Therefore, Grover's algorithm is not a miraculous technique with which to find an item in an unordered set without having to go through it: we could say that it is a sort of indexing technique, which from the point of view of practical use has no advantage to offer with respect to the database management techniques that exist today and are currently in use (and not since computers exist, but since filing cabinets exist).

But beware: admitting that Grover's algorithm is a kind of indexing technique we would still have too high a consideration of it. If we have a database of one million books, and we build a single alphabetically ordered list, then we can use it to perform a binary search for any author: Jones, Smith, etc. The ordered index is always the same for the entire database. But if we wanted to search for Jones with Grover's algorithm, we would have to construct an U_{f0} matrix which exactly matches Jones's search, and if we wanted to search for Smith we should construct an U_{f1} matrix which corresponds to Smith's search, and which is not the same to use for Jones. So we should do the following steps: go through the unsorted database and find Jones; construct U_{f0} which allows to find Jones because it corresponds to Jones's position; finally execute Grover's quantum algorithm which would roughly tell us what we already know exactly because it is the necessary prerequisite to run the algorithm.

This sounds like a comedy, but if you are in doubt, carefully read again the description of Grover's algorithm, and you will be persuaded that this is the case. Grover's algorithm would make sense (neglecting the other problems) only if there were data that are acquired from their sources in the form of U_f matrices ready for the execution of the algorithm: which is a chimera. Grover's algorithm has an aspect of similarity with the search in a database because the black box functions:

bit func(bit vector[N])

must be executed, in the worst case, for all possible arguments to find the returned value, just as an unsorted database must be searched, in the worst case, for all its elements to find one. This is too fragile a resemblance to be the basis for building a useful technology.

6.5 Shor's algorithm

At this point, the four algorithms examined have proved to be of a purely theoretical nature and interest, and whoever wants to find a good reason for the investment of time or capital in the quantum computing project can only hope that the famous Shor algorithm will let us glimpse the perspective of something usable. Let us start with a quotation that, given the authority of the newspaper which it comes from, is a good expression of the reasons why the Shor algorithm is considered so important:

> There is also, in parallel with this race to build better machines, a race to develop useful quantum algorithms to run on them. The most famous example so far is probably Shor's algorithm. This is the piece of quantum–turbocharged maths that allows rapid factorisation of large numbers into their component primes, and thus scares cryptographers, a group whose trade depends on this being a hard thing to do. But if quantum computers are really to earn their keep, then other algorithms will be needed. Developing them will be assisted by the fact that a lot of the proposed applications (drug design, materials science and so on) themselves depend on quantum processes. This, indeed, is why those applications have been so intractable until now.

> *The Economist* September 28th 2019, p. 75

Since the object is the search for the factors of a number, before describing in detail Shor's algorithm, which requires a lot of patience and attention, let us get familiar with a small and very simple algorithm for finding the prime factors of a number, which we need to have a concrete and correct perception of the computational complexity of the problem. Recall that while multiplying two numbers (prime or not) is a simple problem, the inverse problem of finding the factors of a given number is a much more complex problem, both for the human brain and for a computer.

A large number of divisions have to be executed, although to find the prime factors of an integer N it is not necessary to divide it by all integers greater than 1 and less than N: if N=1000, it is immediate and intuitive that 999 cannot be a factor of it, because another *integer* M such that M×999=1000 cannot exist. It is immediate that the maximum integer factor of 1000 is 500, because 500×2=1000, and it is immediate that if the number N is odd, then the maximum integer factor cannot be greater than N/3, because if there were an integer factor M greater than N/3, then there should be another integer factor Z such that Z×M=N: but this factor Z should be an integer greater than 2 and smaller than 3, which obviously does not exists. So, to find the prime factors of a number N, we can run the following algorithm:

- divide N by 2, if the remainder of the division is zero, add 2 to the result list, assign N=N/2 and start again;
- then divide N by A, with A starting at 3 and increasing 2 by 2 not until N, but until the upper limit N/A, for the reason stated above. Whenever the remainder of the division is zero, add A to the result list, assign N=N/A and start again;
- when A exceeds N/A the algorithm is finished. The residual value of N is the last factor.

This algorithm only returns prime factors, because dividing by a non-prime number X never gives remainder zero, because previously the remainder zero would have been obtained by dividing by prime factors of X. That is, division by 9 (even if it is attempted in vain, because the algorithm does not know the list of prime numbers) never gives remainder zero, because the remainder zero would have been found by dividing by 3 and the loop would have started again. If the number N is prime, the algorithm finds nothing and returns N as the only factor. The number of divisions performed is approximately half the square root of N, in the worst case with N prime.

To test the algorithm with large enough numbers, we use the 64-bit integers generally available with the "long long" declaration and define this type:

```
typedef unsigned long long unsigned_64_bit;
```

The function that can factor a 64-bit number, so any decimal with 18 digits (because 2^{64} is greater than 10^{18}), is as follows:

```
void QCF_Non_Shor_factoring_64_bit()
{
unsigned_64_bit a, N;
// input N
N = xxxxxxxx; //some number, max 18 decimal digits
next_test_even:
  a = 2;
  if ( N % a == 0 )
  {
    // output or store a (=2) in the list of factors
    // ...
    N /= a;
    goto next_test_even;
  }
```

```
next_test_odd:
  for ( a = 3; a <= (N/(a)); a += 2 )
  {
    if ( N % a == 0 )
    {
      // output or store a in the list of factors
      // ...
      N /= a;
      goto next_test_odd;
    }
  }
  if ( N > 1 )
  {
    // store N in the list of factors. N is the
    // last factor
    // if this is the only result, N is a
    // prime number
    // ...
  }
}
```

This function could be subject to further optimization, because it has obvious redundancies, however the execution time is very short because it only performs integer increments and divisions. In *QcNooq* 6.5.A you can try to run it with the number B= 757.887.406.446.280.110, which is the product of the prime numbers: $2 \times 3 \times 5 \times 7 \times 11 \times 13 \times 17 \times 19 \times 23 \times 29 \times 31 \times 37 \times 41 \times 47 \times 53$. By adding inside the code a counter of the divisions performed, we see that factoring this number requires 140 divisions and the running time is obviously unnoticeable. The integer B+1 has three prime factors which are found by performing 184,346 divisions. On the other hand, the integer B−1 is a prime number, and this can be ascertained with 435,283,645 integer divisions, for the execution of which a CPU at 2 GHz takes about six seconds (if the program is written in C and compiled with optimization option for the speed of execution, and presumably more time with any other language).

By the way, recall that the microprocessors of the years after 1980 had frequencies measured in MHz, not in GHz: when the idea of quantum computing was born the possibilities offered by the existing hardware were minimal compared to today, and this throws some light on the context of the original idea.

Shor's algorithm, like Grover's, has an external loop that must be performed by the classical computer controlling the process, and an internal loop that will require a lot of resources to be emulated, and which is intended to be performed by a quantum computer. To understand the algorithm it is essential to first execute the outer loop by solving the inner loop with a classic routine, then replace the inner loop with the quantum component of the algorithm. The emulation without the quantum component can be performed on a 16-bit number (or a greater one), while the full emulation, with literal and complete emulation the quantum component, can only be performed on much smaller numbers.

Some preliminary definitions are needed.

▶ First of all, remember that by *modulus* we mean the remainder of an integer division. In the following we shall indicate it with the abbreviation Mod or with the corresponding operator in the C language, which is %. For example, the remainder of the integer division 7/2 is obtained with the instruction: int x=7%2, which returns the remainder 1 in the variable x.

▶ Given a number N, 1 and N are the trivial factors, because 1×N=N. The other factors, prime or non-prime, are non-trivial factors. In the following, speaking of the factors of a number, we shall assume that we are talking about the non-trivial factors, and that the trivial ones are of no interest.

▶ Shor's algorithm is based on the notion of the *period* R of a pair of numbers A and N defined as follows:

- N is an integer greater than 2. In the following we shall require that N is an odd and non-prime positive integer, and having at least two (non-trivial) prime factors different from each other, but for the definition of the period this further condition is not necessary.

- A is an integer between 2 and N–1, which must not be a factor of N and must not have factors that are also factors of N;

- the *period* R (depending on A and N) is the smallest integer for which $A^R\%N=1$ holds.

It is shown that for all values of A that do not contain and are not factors of N there is a period R smaller than N.

Let us now take the number N = 6 as an example. With N = 6, A can be 2,3,4 and 5, but for which values of A and 6 is the period defined? Only for 5, because 2, 3 and 4 are or contain factors of 6. For N=6 and A=5 the period is 2, because $A^R = 5^2 = 25$ and $25\% N = 25\% 6 = 1$.

The period has this denomination because it corresponds to a periodic trend: in fact it is shown that if R is a period of (N,A) and therefore $A^R\% N = 1$, then also raising A to any integer multiple of R and executing the modulus of N the result 1 is obtained.

For example, let us consider N=15 and A=2 for which the period R is 4 (in fact 2^4=16 and 16%15=1). For integer multiples of R we have the following trend:

x	**0**	1	2	3	**4**	5	6	7	**8**
2^x	1	2	4	8	16	32	64	128	256
$2^x\%15$	**1**	2	4	8	**1**	2	4	8	**1**

x	9	10	11	**12**	13	14	15	**16**
2^x	512	1024	2048	4096	8192	16384	32768	65536
$2^x\%15$	2	4	8	**1**	2	4	8	**1**

As we can see in the table, A (which has value 2) raised to 0×R, to 1×R (which is 4), 2×R, 3×R and 4×R etc. and divided by N (which is 15) always gives the remainder equal to 1. If we graphically represent the trend of the powers of $2^x\%15$, we can intuitively see the periodic trend:

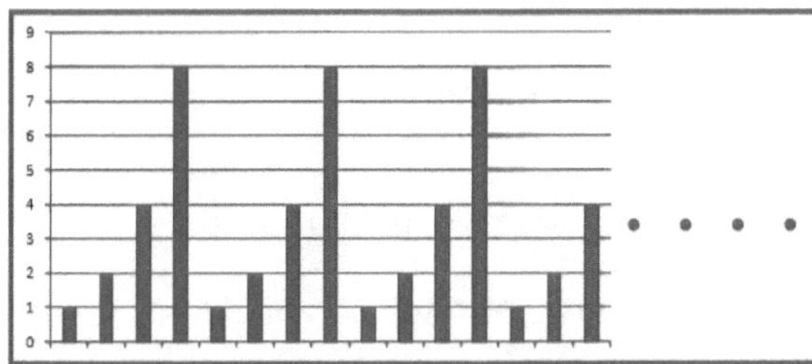

and this allows us to anticipate in a general way the principle of Shor's algorithm: it will first exploit together with $A^x\%N$ another periodic function, which is a certain trigonometric function, to intercept the periods of a number N, and then it will use the properties of the period to derive the factors of N. In a very figurative way, we can say that Shor considers the trend of the $A^x\%N$ function seen as a wave and superimposes another sinusoidal wave to intercept the period values with an interference between waves. This explanation is an extreme simplification, but we need it to enter in the order of ideas of the following.

In *QcNooq* 6.5.C it is possible to search and verify the period for small numbers by performing the calculations entirely for Ax%N. The code uses Euclid's algorithm to find the Greatest Common Divisor (GCD) between two numbers, which is the following:

// Euclid's algorithm for Greatest Common Divisor

```
unsigned short qx_Euclid_GCD_16(unsigned short a,
 unsigned short b)
{
unsigned short r;
  while(b != 0) //repeat until b is reduced to zero
  {
    r = a % b;
    a = b;
    b = r; //swap the role played by a or b
  }
  return a; //... and when b is zero, the GCD is a
}
```

and the code for the period search is as follows:

```
void QCF_do_Shor_Period_16()
{
unsigned short N, A, x;
int R;
double temp;
// assign N
  N = some integer number ...
  for ( A = 2; A < N; ++A )
  {
   R = 0; // flag not found
   for ( x = 0; x < N; ++x )
   {
     temp = pow((double)A, (double)x);
     if (R == 0 &&
       qx_double_equal_enough(fmod(temp, (double)N),
       1.0))
      {
       R = x;
       // display R
      }
   }
   if ( R == 0 ) // no period found for A
   {
     // OK, A is a factor
     if ( qx_Euclid_GCD_16(A,N) != 1 )
     ; // output verification
     else
     ; // output "Software error!";
   }
  }
}
```

The procedure is very simple, following the period definition:

- N is assigned.

- A runs through the values from 2 to N–1.

- in the loop of A, x runs through the values from 2 to N–1.

- the power A^x is executed in floating point (an inelegant technique) and it is checked if the power MOD N is 1: the floating point is indispensable because even for small numbers the powers A^x will exceed the range of integers, and therefore after the elevation at power instead of the integer modulus % it is necessary to use the equivalent function fmod() in floating point; the result is evaluated with qx_double_equal_enough() for the usual approximation problem.

- if a period is found, the period is shown.

- finally, a check: if the period is not found, Euclid's algorithm is used to check that A is a factor of N or contains factors: A does not contain factors of N if the Greatest Common Divisor of A and N is equal to 1. If this were not verified, the software would contain an error.

By means of this elementary procedure one could only search for the period for small numbers, because the powers A^x would soon assume values exceeding the calculable range also in floating point. But the search for the period is possible by exploiting a demonstrable property of numbers, which is:

$$A^x \% N = ((A^{x-1} \% N) \times A) \% N.$$

This allows us to find the period R without incurring overflow. We need to exploit a function:

$$qx\_period\_16(A,N)$$

which we must have care to call only for values of A that do not contain factors of N. The search can be tried with *QcNooq* 6.5.D, and the outer loop is the following, in which A runs through the values from 2 to N–1 and the values for which the GCD is different from 1 are skipped:

```
for ( A = 2; A < N; ++A )
{
 // A contains a factor of N
 if ( qx_Euclid_GCD_16(A,N) != 1 )
 {
  ;// output "A= contains factors of N=,
   // no period";
 }
 else
```

```
{
  R = qx_period_16(A,N);
   // output R
 }
}
```

The period search routine, for 16-bit numbers, is implemented as follows:

```
unsigned short qx_period_16(unsigned short A,
 unsigned short N)
{
unsigned short x;
unsigned int value;// can overflow the 16 bit range

  if ( qx_Euclid_GCD_16(A,N) != 1 )
  {
    ; // output "Application error: Never call
    // qx_period_16() if A is or contains a factor
    //of N "
    return 0xffff;  // SW error: never call without
                    // previous GCD control
  }
  value = 1;  // A pow(0)
  // A pow(x) goes into overflow for small values
  // of A
  // so we exploit the property:
  // (A pow (x)) % N = ((A pow(x-1)%N) * A) % N
  for ( x = 0; x < N; ++x )
  {
    // the modulus operation ensures that value is
    // inside the 16 bit range
    value = value % N; // (A pow (x)) % N
    if ( x > 0 && value == 1 )
      return x;
    // here value can overflow the 16 bit range
    value *= A; // x will be incremented, so this
    // performs (A pow(x-1)%N) * A
  }
  // output "Software error: qx_period_16() must
  // find a period");
  return 0xffff; // Software error: according to
        // the theorem we should never get here
}
```

The loop takes advantage of the property we have seen in this way:

- the variable <u>value</u> is initialized to A^0, i.e. 1. Note that the implementation is for 16-bit numbers, but the variable <u>value</u> is a

32-bit one, because the multiplication value=value*A can exceed the range of 16 bits. The next modulus then brings us back to the 16-bit range.

- x runs through the values from 0 to N–1.
- <u>value</u> is replaced by (value% N). This corresponds to running $A^x\%N$.
- if x is greater than 0 and <u>value</u> is equal to 1, x is the period sought. The routine returns x.
- otherwise <u>value</u> is multiplied by A: since x will be incremented, this corresponds to executing $(A^{x-1}\%N)\times A$.
- x is increased and the loop continues.

Since for all values of A that do not contain and are not factors of N there is a period R smaller than N, if the cycle on the variable x did not find a period, we would have an error in the software implementation. Let us follow the algorithm step by step for the values A=5 and N=6, for which we know that the period is 2 (because $5^2\%6=1$):

x	value	value % N	value * A	decision
0	1	1	5	continue because x == 0
1	5	5	25	continue because value % N not equal to 1
2	25	1		x is the period R, return x

And with this we have the tools to calculate the period R in a classical way.

At this point, we can exploit the properties of the period to retrieve not exactly the prime factors, but some factors of a number using the non-quantum part of Shor's algorithm. Precisely, remember that the non-quantum part uses the properties of the period to find the factors of a number (without being able to tell if they are prime factors or not), while the quantum part uses a quantum circuit to find periods. Therefore, the complete implementation of the algorithm consists in inserting the quantum circuit for the retrieval of the periods inside the external loop that uses the periods. If the purpose is to understand the logic of the algorithm, as we have already said, it is necessary to consider the external loop separately from the internal one.

In the external loop the following rules are applied:

- choose a number N that is odd and has at least two prime factors different from each other (this condition is valid for the complete implementation of the algorithm – by executing only the external non-quantum loop it can be neglected, it will be verified that the algorithm gives the expected results for any positive integer).

- choose a value of A between 2 and N–1. Generally the descriptions of the algorithm suggest to use a random value of A, but to verify the algorithm it is preferable to go through all the values of A, and so we shall do in the implementation.

- use Euclid's algorithm to find the Greatest Common Divisor of A and N. If it is different from 1, then we have found a factor of N, which is the Greatest Common Divisor itself. Always remember: we find a factor, not necessarily a prime factor: the algorithm is not able to distinguish this.

- otherwise find the period R of A and N. This can be done with the quantum circuit, but in the first implementation we shall use the non-quantum method qx_period_16().

- if R is odd, discard A (the algorithm does not work with R odd, to understand the reason it would be necessary to study the complete proofs given by Shor, so let us just accept the rule).

- otherwise use Euclid's algorithm to calculate:

$$GCDA = qx\_Euclid\_GCD\_16((A^{R/2}+1),N)$$

and

$$GCDB = qx\_Euclid\_GCD\_16((A^{R/2}-1),N).$$

- GCDA and GCDB thus calculated are always factors of N. Sometimes they are trivial (1 or N), while sometimes they are non-trivial and then they can be added to the list of factors found.

The code is in *QcNooq* 6.5.E and 6.5.F. Note that the code is not an emulation, but an implementation of the non-quantum part of the algorithm, whose external loop is not intended to be executed by quantum hardware. The code performs the steps described above. The indispensable instructions for the algorithm alone (output is omitted) are the following:

```
void QCF_Non_Quantum_Shor_16()
{
unsigned short k;
unsigned short A, N, GCDA, GCDB, R;
unsigned short A_pow_R_half;
  N = some 16 bit number ...;
  // step 1: we should avoid prime numbers ...
  // ... if needed use QCF_do_factoring_16_bit to
  // detect if N has at least 2 different prime
```

```c
// factors
// step 2: randomly choose A, or let us try all
// the values of A
for ( A = 2; A < N; ++A )
{
  // GCDA > 1 contains factors or is a factor
  if ((GCDA=qx_Euclid_GCD_16(A,N)) != 1 )
  {
    ; // output GCDA in factors list
  }
  else // A is a co-prime of N
  {
    R = qx_period_16(A,N); // a period R exists
    if ( R % 2 == 1 ) // if R is odd discard A
    {
      continue; // discard odd periods
    }
    A_pow_R_half = 1;
    // calculate A pow(R/2)
    for ( k = 0; k < (R/2); ++k )
    {
      A_pow_R_half *= A;
    }
    GCDA = qx_Euclid_GCD_16(A_pow_R_half+1,N);
    GCDB = qx_Euclid_GCD_16(A_pow_R_half-1,N);
    char ga_trivial = ( GCDA == 1 || GCDA == N );
    char gb_trivial = ( GCDB == 1 || GCDB == N );
    if ( !ga_trivial || !gb_trivial )
    {
      if ( !ga_trivial )
      {
        ; // output GCDA in result list
      }
      if ( !gb_trivial )
      {
        ; // output GCDB in result list
      }
    }
    else
    {
      ; // output trivial result
    }
  }
}
```

This code is sufficient to test the outer loop with small numbers. But whoever checked it carefully, would observe that there is a strong limitation: with 16 bits the $A^{R/2}$ power will easily overflow, for numbers that are not very small. For this reason in *QcNooq* there are two variants (not reproduced here):

- QCF_Non_Quantum_Shor_16_overflow_controlled() at point 6.5.E, which uses the floating point for the $A^{R/2}$ power and is the function to be used to check the algorithm's performance with not too small numbers. But the $A^{R/2}$ power can overflow also with the precision of double numbers, and in this case the values of A are discarded.

- QCF_Non_Quantum_Shor_16_overflow_NOT_controlled() which corresponds to the code reproduced here, and in which $A^{R/2}$ will normally overflow. However, just for curiosity it should be observed, that trying to execute both routines with numbers of 3 or 4 decimal digits, the algorithm gives correct results (returns factors of N) even when $A^{R/2}$ overflows: this is a consequence of the fact that the algorithm is based on the properties of the modulus operations.

Furthermore, the actual implementation in *QcNooq* uses our elementary prime factorization function for each factor found to indicate the prime factors of the factor found by Shor: this part is foreign to Shor's algorithm, and we add it only to facilitate the interpretation and verification of the output.

Quantum part of Shor's algorithm

Shor's algorithm requires that the number N to which it applies is odd and has two different prime factors. The smallest number to which Shor applies is therefore 15, because odd numbers less than 15 are all prime, except 9, which does not have two different prime factors.

We proceed in this way:

- it is necessary to perform $A^M \% N$ with $0 \leq A < N$ and with $0 \leq M < N$ by means of a quantum circuit. We must therefore build a U_f matrix of adequate size to be allowed to perform:

Step: 0	1	2
$|x\rangle$	[U_f]	$|x\rangle$
$|y\rangle$		$|y\wedge f(x)\rangle = |y\wedge f(A,M,N)\rangle = |y\wedge(A^M\%N)\rangle$

where, as always, $|x\rangle$ and $|y\rangle$ are vectors and represent all possible values of the input and output. Observe that the output $|y\rangle$ serves to represent a number whose dimension is N, but $|x\rangle$ must represent all arrangements of A and M (dispositions with repetition), and therefore the dimension of the vector $|x\rangle$ is the square of that of $|y\rangle$. Precisely, for a number N whose factors we want to find, the dimension of the vector $|x\rangle$ is d×d and that of $|y\rangle$ is d, where d is equal to N if N is a power of 2, otherwise it is the next power of 2. So, for example, for N=8 we have d=8, but for N=9 we have d=16. We shall see shortly the reason.

The reader may object here: but so even for very small numbers we shall have to deal with gigantic matrices. Is this algorithm feasible? Well, the doubt is legitimate, but let us leave such considerations at the end of the work of implementing Shor's algorithm.

- in input we need a vector $|\varphi\rangle$ on which the following operations are performed:

- the part $|x\rangle$ is superposed with the usual Hadamard matrix;

- we act on the whole $|\varphi\rangle$ with the matrix U_f;

- we act on $|x\rangle$ with an operator that we shall call QFT and that we shall describe shortly;

- measurement is performed, and so a measured state is obtained;

- from the measured state the values of A and M are extracted, and now the component A×M of the measured state has a high probability of returning an integer multiple of a period of N;

- therefore to pass from A×M to the period of N, a certain non-quantum algorithm called "continued fractions algorithm" is performed;

- having a period, we go back to the external non-quantum algorithm and find GCDA and GCDB as described above.

The mentioned "continued fractions algorithm" has a certain probability, but not certainty, of returning a period of the number N, and therefore the algorithm must be run several times. Note that the possibility of finding the period given a multiple of it exists because we are dealing with integer numbers: if we were dealing with real numbers there would be no way to solve the equation period=A×M/x without knowing x.

So the general scheme of the quantum part is as follows:

Step:	0	1	2	3	4
x[d×d]	x=|0[d×d]⟩	$[H]^{\otimes d\times d}$	$[U_f]$	[QFT]	[M]
y[d]	y=|0[d]⟩	$[I_d]$		$[I_d]$	
Output	φ_0	φ_1	φ_2	φ_3	

or:

$$([QFT] \otimes [I]_d)\, U_f\, ([H]^{\otimes d\times d} \otimes [I]_d)\, |0[d\times d],0[d]\rangle$$

or:

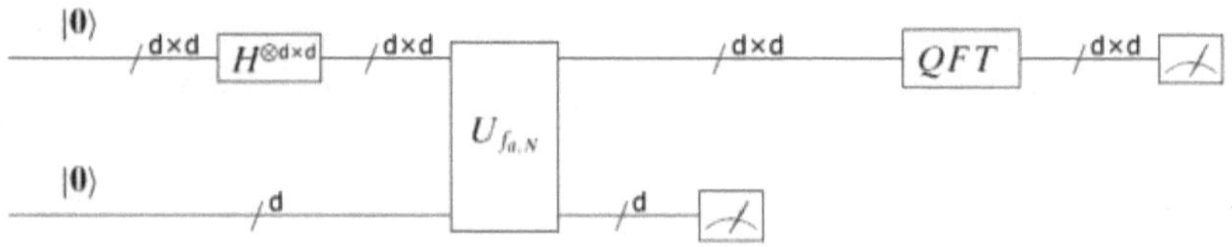

and then the measurement is followed by the non-quantum part consisting of the continued fractions algorithm.

Now we shall implement the emulation of the actually quantum part, and for the rest we shall limit ourselves to counting the frequency of the integer multiples of the periods of N=15, which are 2 and 4, in the measurements, thus verifying that the algorithm has a certain probability of returning the periods and therefore some factors of N=15. We shall not implement the continued fractions algorithm because it would be a pure arithmetic exercise: whoever wants to implement it will find its description[1] in the literature.

The first thing to do now is to build the U_f matrix and verify that through it we can perform the operation $A^M\%N$. Let us always recall that in the following the input generically indicated with $|x\rangle$ corresponds to a pair of numbers A and M.

The matrix U_f is a square matrix U_f[d×d×d][d×d×d], where as we have already said d is equal to N if N is a power of 2, otherwise it is the next power of 2. The reason is explained by an example. With N=3 at first sight we could think to compose the matrix with d=N=3, therefore U_f[3×3×3][3×3×3], in this way:

---

[1] Nielsen & Chuang, p. 230.

			A	0	0	0	0	0	0	...	2	2	2
			M	0	0	0	1	1	1	...	2	2	2
A	M	y	f(A,M)^y	0	1	2	0	1	2	...	0	1	2
0	0	0											
0	0	1											
0	0	2											
0	1	0											
0	1	1											
0	1	2											
...	...	...											
2	2	0											
2	2	1											
2	2	2											

Now, for N=3, A=0, M=0 and y={0,1,2} the values of the function are:

N=3	A	M	y	f(A,M)	f(A,M)^y
binary	00	00	00	01	01
decimal	0	0	0	1	1
binary	00	00	01	01	00
decimal	0	0	1	1	0
binary	00	00	10	01	11
decimal	0	0	2	1	**3**

The value of $(A^M\%N)^y$ for y=2 is 3, so the result for y=2 should be represented by the value 1 in the row corresponding to A=0, M=0 and y=2 and in column 3. But the values of f(x)^y for A=0 and M=0 must be represented in columns 0 or 1 or 2, because columns 3, 4 and 5 are reserved for the values of f(x)^y for A=0 and M=1. The representation in column 3 would invade the space reserved for the values for the next M, as we can see by considering the first rows and columns of the matrix:

			a	0	0	0	0	1	0
			x	0	0	0	0	1	1
a	x	y	f(x)^y	0	1	2	0	1	2
0	0	0				1			
0	0	1			1				
0	0	2						**1**	
0	1	0							
0	1	1							
0	1	2							

where the bold 1 is in the illegal column. The consequences would be that the representation would be ambiguous, that the matrix would not be unitary, and that for a=N−1 and M=N−1 some values would go into the columns with index $N^3+f(x)^\wedge y$, when the total number of the columns is N^3. For this reason the matrix must be constructed taking as basis N if N is a power of 2, otherwise the next power. When N is a power of 2 the invasion of the incorrect column to the right does not occur, because the number N in the binary representation contains only one leading 1 followed by zeros, and therefore $f(A,M)^\wedge y$ cannot give a decimal value greater than y.

Expecting to work with 4-bit numbers, the construction of the U_f matrix takes place with these instructions (*QcNooq* 6.5.G).

- Data to work on sized as needed:

```
static qx Ufunc_4_bit[16*16*16*16*16*16];
static qx phi0[16*16*16];
static qx output4_calc_Uf[16*16*16];
```

- Size of the vector needed to host A, M and y:

```
byte N_ceiling;
// ceiling of 2 pow(log base 2 of N) (so assigned
// for readability - should be calculated)
if ( N <= 2 ) N_ceiling = 2;
else if ( N <= 4 ) N_ceiling = 4;
else if ( N <= 8 ) N_ceiling = 8;
else N_ceiling = 16;
```

- Construction of the matrix U_f:

```
for ( A = 0; A < N_ceiling; ++A )
{
  for ( M = 0; M < N_ceiling; ++M )
  {
    // calculation of AM%N
    fx = (byte)qx_a_powx_modN_16(A,M,N);
    for ( y = 0; y < N_ceiling; ++y )
    {
      fx_xor_y = fx^y;
      row =
        ((int)A*N_ceiling*N_ceiling+(int)M*N_ceiling+(
        int)y);
      col =
        ((int)A*N_ceiling*N_ceiling+(int)M*N_ceiling+
        (int)fx_xor_y;
      if ( col >= A*N_ceiling*N_ceiling+M*N_ceiling +
        N_ceiling )
      {
        non_reversible_matrix = 1;
        // check overflow - WARN software error
        if ( col >= N_ceiling*N_ceiling*N_ceiling )
```

```
        continue;
      }
    Ufunc_4_bit[row*(N_ceiling*N_ceiling*N_ceiling)
      +col].a = 1.0;
    }
  }
}
```

Notice that in the construction of U_f, to calculate $A^M\%N$ we used the following function, exploiting the technique we know to avoid numbers out of range:

```
extern unsigned short qx_a_powx_modN_16 (unsigned
 short a, unsigned short x, unsigned short N)
{
unsigned short k;
unsigned int value;// can overflow the 16 bit range
  value = 1;
  // a pow(x) goes into overflow for small values
  // of a
  // so we exploit the property:
  // (a pow (x)) % N = ( (a pow(x-1)%N) * a ) % N
  for ( k = 0; k < x; ++k )
  {
   value = value % N;
   // here it could overflow the 16 bit range
   value *= a;
  }
  return (value % N);
}
```

Before using the matrix for Shor's emulation, let us check that the matrix is constructed correctly. To do this, we first calculate all the values of $A^M\%N$ using the qx_period_16() function:

```
qx display_normal[16]; // type is qx just for
 display
for ( A = 0; A < N; ++A )
{
  // store periods for every A
  if ( qx_Euclid_GCD_16(A,N) == 1 )
   a_known_periods[A] = (byte)qx_period_16(A,N);
  else
   a_known_periods[A] = 0;
  // calculation with simple technique for check
  for ( M = 0; M < N; ++M )
  {
   display_normal[M].a = qx_a_powx_modN_16(A,M,N);
    display_normal[M].b = 0;
```

```
    }
  // display result in vector display_normal
}
```

Then we compute all values of $A^M\%N$ using the matrix U_f. Recall that $|y\rangle$ can have any value in the range allowed for the output, so we give $|y\rangle$ each time a different value, which can be random. So we run through the allowed values of A and M, we give y a random value (if desired, we could add an internal cycle for all the admitted values of y), and we construct φ_0 by resetting it and assigning:

```
phi0[((int)A*N_ceiling*N_ceiling+(int)M*N_ceiling+(
 int)y)].a = 1.0;
```

and finally we multiply $U_f{*}\varphi_0$ and extract the value of $(A^M\%N)\char94 y$ from the resulting vector. The values of $(A^M\% N)$ are obtained from:

```
fx = fx_xor_y^y
```

and are accumulated in the vector intended for the display, which must exhibit a result equal to that obtained with the previous test. The code is:

```
qx display_uf[16]; // type is qx just for display
// this code to calculate periods and to display
// and check Uf :
for ( A = 0; A < N; ++A )
{
  y = qx_random() % N_ceiling;
  // y can have any value
  for ( M = 0; M < N_ceiling; ++M )
  {
    memset(phi0, 0, sizeof(phi0));
    phi0[((int)A*N_ceiling*N_ceiling+(int)M*N_ceilin
     g+(int)y)].a = 1.0;
    qx_matrix_mmul(N_ceiling*N_ceiling*N_ceiling,N_c
     eiling*N_ceiling*N_ceiling,1,(qx
     *)Ufunc_4_bit,phi0,output4_calc_Uf );
    // get the row of output having non zero value
    wz =
     qx_check_measured_state(N_ceiling*N_ceiling*N_c
     eiling, output4_calc_Uf);
    // get the column with the y values
    fx_xor_y = wz % N_ceiling;
    fx = fx_xor_y^y;
    display_uf[M].a = fx; display_uf[M].b = 0;
  }
  // display result in vector display_uf
}
```

In order to allow complete verification, the code in *QcNooq* 6.5.G at the end also calculates the values of $A^M \% N\_ceiling$ (instead of N), i.e. for the entire U_f matrix.

At this point, to fully execute the quantum part, the QFT operator is missing. This operator, where QFT stands for "Quantum Fourier Transform", consists of a matrix of dimensions equal to the dimension of the input $= |x\rangle$, which as we know contains all the allowed values of A and M. The matrix is called the Vandermonde matrix. It assigns a value to the coefficient of the real and imaginary parts of each element and, given the dimension d of the matrix, it can be constructed by assigning to each element of index j, k these values:

QFT[j][k].a = cos(2×π×j×k) / d;

QFT[j][k].b = sin(2×π×j×k) / d;

The code that initializes the matrix in qx_matrix_constant(), given as a parameter the base address <u>dd</u> of the matrix and the size, is therefore:

```
#define QX_C_PIGRECO 3.141592653358979323846
case QX_M22_VANDERMONDE:
  for ( j = 0; j < dimension; ++j )
  {
    for ( k = 0; k < dimension; ++k )
    {
      dd[(j*dimension)+k].a =
       cos((2.0*QX_C_PIGRECO*(double)(j*k))/
       (double)dimension);
      dd[(j*dimension)+k].b =
       sin((2.0*QX_C_PIGRECO*(double)(j*k))/
       (double)dimension);
    }
  }
```

Let us now try to picture what happens. To keep both feet on the ground, remember that hardware can implement U_f matrices because the bits represented in the qubits of the initial state vector can be put in a different state from the initial one by certain physical actions. These can be combined together in such a way as to physically act on the initial system with probabilities of modifying it which are represented by the corresponding matrices U_f, and in this way in the hardware changes occur in the physical state of the components which correspond to the arithmetic operation of multiplying the matrix U_f for the state vector. Using the elementary universal gates it is possible to compose both the matrix that implements $A^M \% N$, and the one corresponding to Vandermonde. The algorithm, as we know from the steps described above, acts like this:

- takes as input a value φ of $|x\rangle$ and $y\rangle$ which can be $|0\rangle$, but also some other (we could look for the optimal value);
- creates the superposition with the Hadamard matrix;
- acts on the vector φ with the matrix that implements $A^M\%N$;
- acts on the vector φ with the Vandermonde matrix.

But the function $A^M\%N$ has a periodic trend, as we know, and the function represented by the Vandermonde matrix, being a trigonometric function, has in turn a periodic trend. If we develop Vandermonde for size 16, and isolate only the real part of the elements, we obtain:

1	1	1	1	1	1	1	1	1	1	1	1	1	1	1	1
1	0,92	0,7	0,38	0	-0,38	-0,7	-0,92	-1	-0,92	-0,7	-0,38	0	0,38	0,7	0,92
1	0,7	0	-0,7	-1	-0,7	0	0,7	1	0,7	0	-0,7	-1	-0,7	0	0,7
1	0,38	-0,7	-0,92	0	0,92	0,7	-0,38	-1	-0,38	0,7	0,92	0	-0,92	-0,7	0,38
1	0	-1	0	1	0	-1	0	1	0	-1	0	1	0	-1	0
1	-0,38	-0,7	0,92	0	-0,92	0,7	0,38	-1	0,38	0,7	-0,92	0	0,92	-0,7	-0,38
1	-0,7	0	0,7	-1	0,7	0	-0,7	1	-0,7	0	0,7	-1	0,7	0	-0,7
1	-0,92	0,7	-0,38	0	0,38	-0,7	0,92	-1	0,92	-0,7	0,38	0	-0,38	0,7	-0,92
1	-1	1	-1	1	-1	1	-1	1	-1	1	-1	1	-1	1	-1
1	-0,92	0,7	-0,38	0	0,38	-0,7	0,92	-1	0,92	-0,7	0,38	0	-0,38	0,7	-0,92
1	-0,7	0	0,7	-1	0,7	0	-0,7	1	-0,7	0	0,7	-1	0,7	0	-0,7
1	-0,38	-0,7	0,92	0	-0,92	0,7	0,38	-1	0,38	0,7	-0,92	0	0,92	-0,7	-0,38
1	0	-1	0	1	0	-1	0	1	0	-1	0	1	0	-1	0
1	0,38	-0,7	-0,92	0	0,92	0,7	-0,38	-1	-0,38	0,7	0,92	0	-0,92	-0,7	0,38
1	0,7	0	-0,7	-1	-0,7	0	0,7	1	0,7	0	-0,7	-1	-0,7	0	0,7
1	0,92	0,7	0,38	0	-0,38	-0,7	-0,92	-1	-0,92	-0,7	-0,38	0	0,38	0,7	0,92

which obviously has a periodic trend, as well as the coefficients of the imaginary part also have. Now, after the action with the Hadamard matrix, as we know, every possible value of the output vector has the same probability of being measured. Acting with U_f of $A^M\%N$ and then with Vandermonde, instead, it happens that *the probability is increased that the measured value is a multiple of a period of the number N*, from which a factor of N can then be obtained. This is the key to the algorithm: the increase in the probability of measuring a multiple of a period (directly a period would be preferable, but an algorithm that is capable of this has not been found).

Thus, the result is obtained as a consequence of the properties of both these numerical functions ($A^M\%N$ and the Fourier transformation implemented by the Vandermonde matrix), and the rigorous proof, developed by Shor, can be found as always in the complete discussions.

We can move on to the emulation of the procedure, which at this point consists of the usual steps: initialization of the input vector, construction of the necessary constant matrices, multiplication and measurement.

For N=15, we know that the base dimension we need to refer to is 16, and so we need the matrices:

```
qx phi0[16*16*16];  // input φ₀
qx Ufunc_4_bit[16*16*16*16*16*16];  // for Aᴹ%N
qx UQTFN[16*16*16*16];  // Vandermonde for |x> = A,M
qx HADAN[16*16*16*16];  // Hadamard for |x> = A,M
qx IDEN [16*16];  // Identity for |y>
qx UQTFIDE[16*16*16*16*16*16];  // Vandermonde
                                // tensor Identity
qx HADAIDE[16*16*16*16*16*16];  // Hadamard tensor
                                // Identity
qx phi1[16*16*16];  // φ₁
qx phi2[16*16*16];  // φ₂
qx phi3[16*16*16];  // φ₃
qx measured[16*16*16];  // measured φ
```

U_f is initialized with the code seen above to verify U_f. the vector φ0 takes the values |x⟩=|0⟩ and |y⟩=|0⟩, and therefore:

```
memset(phi0, 0, sizeof(phi0));
phi0[0].a = 1.0;
// if index==0 then |x>=|0>, |y>=|0>,
```

The other necessary matrices are constructed with the initialization function of constant matrices, which by our convention requires as a parameter the base 2 logarithm of the dimension, and therefore we have:

```
hdva_size_log = 8; iden_size_log = 4;
qx_matrix_constant(QX_M22_VANDERMONDE,hdva_size_log
,UQTFN);
qx_matrix_constant(QX_M22_HADA,hdva_size_log,HADAN)
;
qx_matrix_constant(QX_M22_IDEN,iden_size_log,IDEN);
```

The overall matrices are constructed with the tensor product:

```
qx_matrix_tensor_product(N_ceiling*N_ceiling,N_ceil
ing*N_ceiling,N_ceiling,N_ceiling, HADAN, IDEN,
HADAIDE );
qx_matrix_tensor_product(N_ceiling*N_ceiling,N_ceil
ing*N_ceiling,N_ceiling,N_ceiling, UQTFN, IDEN,
UQTFIDE );
```

and at this point we have all the elements to perform:

$$([QFT] \otimes [I]_d) \, U_f \, ([H]^{\otimes d \times d} \otimes [I]_d) \, |0[d \times d],0[d]\rangle$$

which is implemented by:

```
qx_matrix_mmul(N_ceiling*N_ceiling*N_ceiling,N_ceil
 ing*N_ceiling*N_ceiling,1,(qx *)HADAIDE,phi0,phi1
 );
qx_matrix_mmul(N_ceiling*N_ceiling*N_ceiling,N_ceil
 ing*N_ceiling*N_ceiling,1,(qx
 *)Ufunc_4_bit,phi1,phi2 );
qx_matrix_mmul(N_ceiling*N_ceiling*N_ceiling,N_ceil
 ing*N_ceiling*N_ceiling,1,(qx *)UQTFIDE,phi2,phi3
 );
```

Now we can perform the measurement and extract the result. This operation can be repeated many times by measuring <u>phi3</u> and bringing the result in <u>measured</u>, because we are in emulation (remember instead that with real hardware we could measure only once, and then we should repeat the procedure from the beginning). From the measured vector we can extract the values of A and M:

```
byte N_ceiling, A, M, y;
unsigned int AMy;
qx_state_measurement(N_ceiling*N_ceiling*N_ceiling,
 phi3,measured );
AMy =
 qx_check_measured_state(N_ceiling*N_ceiling*N_ceil
 ing, measured);
A = AMy/(N_ceiling*N_ceiling);
M = (AMy/(N_ceiling))%N_ceiling;
AM = A*M;
```

Now let us consider the product A×M by remembering that the periods of 15 are 4 and 2. If we perform the measurement a certain number of times (for example, a thousand), we shall see that the frequency with which we extract a multiple of 4 is greater than the expected result in the case in which we performed the simple superposition with Hadamard. We should therefore fix the desired number of measurements and perform:

```
for ( measurement_no = 0; measurement_no <
 number_of_loops; ++measurement_no )
{
  qx_state_measurement(N_ceiling*N_ceiling*N_ceilin
   g,phi3,measured );
  AMy =
   qx_check_measured_state(N_ceiling*N_ceiling*N_ce
   iling, measured);
  A = AMy/(N_ceiling*N_ceiling);
```

```
  M = (AMy/(N_ceiling))%N_ceiling;
  AM = A*M;
  ++A_M_occurrences[AM];
  // count periods of N=15
  if ( (AM) % 4 == 0 ) ++A_M_multiples_of_4;
  else if ( (AM) % 2 == 0 ) ++A_M_multiples_of_2;
  else ++A_M_not_useful;
}
```

and then evaluate the frequency of the multiples of period 4 in the counter A_M_multiples_of_4.

At this point we could perform the procedure corresponding to the continued fractions algorithm to derive the period 4 from its multiples, and then insert ourselves into the outer loop to derive the factors of N, but this would be a simple arithmetic exercise with no relation to quantum computing.

Comment on Shor's algorithm

That Shor's algorithm cannot have any practical use, it is obvious: quantum hardware is not capable of calculating $A^x\%N$, and therefore it is necessary to provide its values in the form of a matrix U_f containing all the values of $A^x\%N$ for $0 \leq A < N$ and $0 \leq x < N$. The elementary algorithm we saw initially finds the prime factors of N with a number of integer divisions equal to at most half of $\sqrt{N}$ and without the need for any support matrix, while here we should perform a certain operation (heavier than a division) for a number of times equal to N^2, and compile a giant-sized matrix. With this we would have done only part of the work: then with complex techniques we would arrive at approximating the factors of the number N, and in this the quantum part of the algorithm would be advantageous just because it would perform with a single action each of the three multiplications of the expression :

$$([QFT] \otimes [I]_d)\, U_f\, ([H]^{\otimes d \times d} \otimes [I]_d)\, |0[d \times d], 0[d]\rangle.$$

whose setup would cost an amount of work unmanageable in reality. The algorithm therefore has the value of a theoretical prototype and nothing more (without the need to mention that when we calculate $A^x\%N$ sometimes we would encounter the result=1, and so we would know that the current value of x is a period without need of the quantum component).

The most important observation, however, is not this, but is that despite all its complexity, Shor's algorithm does not reveal any potential of a quantum computer as a programmable machine capable of solving a generality of problems. The simpler algorithms compared to Shor are only capable of extracting, with approximations, what has been previously calculated in the U_f matrices, and the difference of the Shor algorithm compared to the others is only that it exploits certain specific properties of the hardware to find the numerical values of a precise function, resulting from the successive multiplication of the $A^x \% N$ matrix and of the Vandermonde matrix which implements the Fourier transformation. The situation is similar to that of someone loading a cannon, adjusting the elevation and firing: after firing he could go to see where the grenade fell and could claim to have calculated a numerical value of the function that describes the trajectory of a bullet: in a certain sense the assertion is true, but then, apart from the objection that to prepare the shot you need the firing tables in which the solution to the problem sought is already given, what would the gunner answer, if we asked him what other function we could calculate besides that of the ballistics of a cannon? There would be no answer, just as, at this point, we have no idea of the use we could make of quantum computers, even with respect to very simple problems, brilliantly solved by the "classical" computer we are used to.

Finally, note that Shor's algorithm, as it resembles the algorithm implemented with the firing of a cannon, resembles that of Simon that we have seen above: both use the wave functions of quantum phenomena to drop a kind of a bullet in order to reveal, very approximately, a periodicity, without indicating any way out for an effective use of the instrument as a general calculator.

7. Perspectives of quantum computing

7.1 Useful algorithms and state of the art

In all likelihood, at this point, readers find themselves deeply disoriented and disappointed with respect to the expectations they placed in the matter. Once the structure is understood, quantum algorithms seem to be just interesting exercises for the mathematician studying the properties of certain numerical functions, but nothing that has to do with computer technology. They are unable to do other than return, moreover approximately, some information that the setup necessary for execution must find by classical means before starting to execute the algorithms, and all the work currently done around quantum computing appears something desperately senseless, because the operations necessary to execute the algorithms employ monstrous computational resources to find the solution of tiny problems by redundant means, which the quantum algorithms will only repeat. We have examined in depth three algorithms (Deutsch's, DJ and Grover's) that are capable to repeat like parrots, and with approximation, what already results exactly from the setup necessary to execute them, and two algorithms (Simon's and Shor's) that after a gigantic setup manage to perform a semblance of approximate calculation by exploiting certain wave interferences, without therefore indicating any useful methodology for using quantum hardware as a general purpose computer.

It is for this reason that we have indicated in the introduction of this book the most rigorous sources to refer to in order to deepen the subject. If the quantum computing project is close to your heart, and if what you know now is a disappointment that drives you to doubt, consider the possibility that this book is wrong, use what you have learned from reading this book to study the subject with greater rigor starting from the suggested texts, and finally judge with your intelligence if there is any possibility of using a quantum computer satisfactorily, or if the project is what it appears given what we now know about algorithms, that is, the result of a simplistic leap from the theoretical principles of quantum mechanics to those of an imaginary technology.

But now, before discussing the necessary conclusions that follow from the point of view of this book, let us make a small clarification on:

7.2 Quantum programming languages

With all that we have seen, it is easy to understand that it is possible to design quantum programming languages with which to express feasible operations. There will be four basic classes of instructions:

1. Instructions for the classical computer that will control the calls to the quantum processor in external loops, in algorithms such as Grover's and Shor's; there will be nothing here unlike any programming language.

2. Instructions for the initialization of qubit vectors.

3. Instructions for acting on qubit vectors by means of matrices. For this purpose it will be necessary to compose the matrices, and in this regard let us take into account what we have mentioned above, in section 5.3: it is shown that there are sets of basic gates (corresponding to physical actions that hardware can perform) that allow the composition of configurations equivalent to any unitary matrix, such as:

$$\{\text{Hadamard},\ R_\theta,\ I_n,\ \text{controlled–NOT}\}.$$

The implementation of a language will be based on this or another universal set and will allow its application, using instructions allowing to invoke universal gates.

4. Measurement instructions.

Of these points, the third contains a huge new problem, which perhaps has arisen by itself in the reader's mind: the development of a matrix to represent a U_f function in theory is always feasible by means of a rather simple software, which will apply the definition of the problem to be solved, and will be hampered only by the immense dimensions reached by data; but once we have developed a matrix of considerable size to represent any U_f function, to implement it in quantum hardware we must represent it with the set of available gates, corresponding to the implementable physical actions, and this is no trivial problem. In fact, only for very small matrices currently exist deterministic and univocal rules for the conversion into the gates of the available universal set, while for matrices of more considerable size a new problem of high complexity opens up, of which it would be necessary to seek the solution. But given the upstream problem of the size of the matrices themselves, it will probably never be necessary to deal with this derivative problem.

And with this we say no more about languages: the reader who has the desire can easily read up on the languages that have been implemented, without encountering any obstacle to their understanding, and could also define a quantum language, implement it with the basic libraries of *QcNooq* and verify the correctness of the implementation with the quantum algorithms discussed in the previous chapter. It remains to be established what use can ever be made of these languages.

7.3 A brief history of the quantum computing project

As for the state of the art regarding quantum algorithms and their application, the picture is disconcerting: quantum algorithms seem the result of clutching at straws to pretend that a hardware tool that does not have the characteristics of a computer can be considered such, deceiving oneself thanks to the satisfaction out of the great structural complexity of the algorithms themselves and the underlying physics. It is not easy to accept the idea that the current climate of euphoria around quantum computing, and the millionaire investments that are being made (in the year 2020 a billion dollars, we read in specialized newspapers and web pages), are focused on the attempt to build a machine which, once built and functioning, and of any size, therefore equipped with a thousand or a million or a billion efficient qubits, would only serve to give superficially tautological answers with respect to the input. Yet, the readers of this book could have an inkling that the matter did not add up when they discovered, in section 4.4 above, that it takes not 8 but $2^8=256$ qubits to emulate a qubyte: this was enough to suspect an unmanageable combinatorial explosion of data, which is then fully confirmed by the reality of quantum algorithms.

To focus on the fundamental handicap, let us remember that to deal with two bits it is necessary to develop the table of the four possible cases, and that to study the behaviour of N bits, 2^N numbers are needed. Therefore to analyze a problem involving 32 bits we need vectors of size 2^{32}, that is 4,294,967,296, and square matrices reaching 2^{2N}. This without doubt cannot be avoided, however it concerns the study, design and emulation of quantum algorithms, not the functionality of the hardware itself: in quantum hardware there would be 32 qubits to represent 32 bits, nothing more than that. So now it might occur to us that if somehow we could jump directly to the composition of quantum gates, without developing the tables of

U_f matrices and other transformations, the combinatorial explosion problem would cease to exist. We will talk about this shortly.

But if the combinatorial explosion is the first factor we become aware of, then, by studying the algorithms, we realize the second as well: as we know, a quantum computer can neither copy a variable, nor perform a test on two variables and jump to another program location, and in the absence of these two features it cannot work similarly to a classical computer, or to a Turing machine. In reality, somehow it could do it, because by introducing the necessary redundancies, it is possible to create reversible versions of all the logic gates: only if we took this path, we would then have a quantum replica of the Turing machine, we would again have a computer that would work by breaking down the problems in minimum units of information and would treat them in sequence, and it would be necessary to demonstrate that such a quantum technology full of redundancies to realize a computer that works in sequence would be advantageous compared to the electronics used up to now. The original idea of performing parallel calculations by exploiting the peculiar characteristics of quantum phenomena would be completely lost from sight. But the initial intentions were completely different: the quantum computer should have worked performing parallel calculations thanks to entanglement and superposition, which are the hallmark of quantum hardware. Only, as far as we know now there is no method to really use them as the principle of an alternative way of performing calculations: entanglement and superposition are physical phenomena, by performing which we can obtain certain values of the functions that describe them for given arguments, and this is what happens inside Simon's and Shor's algorithms, which at most resemble a little a slide rule, which by putting two logarithmic scales near to each other allows the immediate reading of the result of infinite multiplications and divisions, and therefore in a certain sense creates a superposition (however, it is a very efficient hardware). The other algorithms that we have studied are limited to building a quantum gate dedicated to the problem, and with a certain fun, they obtain approximate results when a gate implemented with common electronics would obtain exact results.

The whole affair seems an immense misunderstanding, but things are as we have described them, and those who can see the problem as a whole know this clearly, while probably the specialists who have limited knowledge of particular aspects of the question, related to the physics of hardware or linear algebra, are also aware of the problem, but they remain entangled in muddled thinking about the whole. However, it seems a mystery that so much energy can be invested in the construction of a machine whose theoretical design is so disappointing: and therefore we must try to get an idea of the way in which specialists who have a complete overview of the problem see the question.

The fundamental texts from which we drew the information necessary to put this book together in some corner of the discussion express this state of affairs with a certain sincerity, albeit incidentally and without insisting too much. Yanofsky and Mannucci's book comes to the subject in the course of a chapter (the seventh) in which, after having described the five algorithms in the same order followed by us, the structure of quantum programming languages is discussed in some detail, and it is here that readers stumble upon this observation (on page 233) as if by chance:

> The trick described earlier has two main costs:
>
> ■ The reversibilization operation we performed by hand requires explicit calculations of f on all the input values, and the table grows exponentially in the size of the input. That is, of course, unacceptable because such a preprocessing would erode all the benefits of quantum speedup (not to mention the unpleasant fact that to carry out simple arithmetical operations via Uf, we must already compute all f's values!).
>
> ■ The extra qubits one needs to allocate. As it stands, it could create a big quantum memory issue, in case we needed to carry out several operations in a row.

This summary is very clear and corresponds exactly to the conclusions reached by studying the algorithms: on the one hand the memory required for the setup of any useful algorithm is not manageable, on the other hand the setup work prior to an algorithm would perform the output calculation on its own. The absurdity of the situation, and the embarrassment, are expressed in the fact that this is a unique and marginal observation in the book: notice that what is designated as "the trick described earlier" is nothing else than the fundamental construction technique of reversible matrices U_f: the attempt to play down the problem through the rhetorical expedient of understatement, which alludes to a fundamental aspect qualifying it as an accessory "trick", is obvious. But readers who have carefully followed the development of the book are only confirmed by what they have understood for themselves, namely that the setup of a quantum software would require the support of a classical computer with dimensions outside of reality, and then the work done would be useless. The passage is followed by a hint to techniques with which the two problems could be made a little less dramatic, not without the use of an ironic register which is another fig leaf in the face of the embarrassment for the situation, characterized by the incidental words: "A bit cumbersome, isn't it?" (p. 234). In short, the book by Yanofsky and Mannucci knows very well that we have nothing in hand, and with this flash of sincerity, if nothing else, it confirms the doubt of the readers, who otherwise might think that they have not penetrated the matter due to their own limits of intelligence and knowledge of the prerequisites, as often happens. But excepting this no other light is shed on the problem.

Nielsen and Chuang's book, on the other hand, talks about this in the very first introductory pages, and after presenting Shor's and Grover's algorithms as two successful examples, it observes on page 7:

> What other problems can quantum computers solve more quickly than classical computers? The short answer is that we don't know. Coming up with good quantum algorithms seems to be hard. A pessimist might think that's because there's nothing quantum computers are good for other than the applications already discovered! We take a different view. Algorithm design for quantum computers is hard because designers face two difficult problems not faced in the construction of algorithms for classical computers. First, our human intuition is rooted in the classical world. If we use that intuition as an aid to the construction of algorithms, then the algorithmic ideas we come up with will be classical ideas. To design good quantum algorithms one must 'turn off' one's classical intuition for at least part of the design process, using truly quantum effects to achieve the desired algorithmic end. Second, to be truly interesting it is not enough to design an algorithm that is merely quantum mechanical. The algorithm must be *better* than any existing classical algorithm! Thus, it is possible that one may find an algorithm which makes use of truly quantum aspects of quantum mechanics, that is nevertheless not of widespread interest because classical algorithms with comparable performance characteristics exist. The combination of these two problems makes the construction of new quantum algorithms a challenging problem for the future.

Here the argument at first glance seems closer to the psychology of Ixion, deceived by Jupiter, who tried to embrace a cloud believing it to be the woman he was in love with. The authors' argument is: we have conceived a machine with immense potential, without yet being able to build it, nevertheless we have precisely defined the behaviour of the equivalent theoretical machine; if we cannot find a way to use it, it is because our minds are still rooted in ancient, "classical" habits; when we get rid of them, we shall also know how to design truly quantum algorithms for quantum computers. However (we add), miraculously we managed to design the hardware. It is therefore not clear why the emancipated minds that have been able to design the machine should also not be able to think about what it can serve: but probably, in the authors' thinking, the emancipation of the mind from "classical" perspectives is a gradual process. Notice, in detail, that in the expression "what other problems" the word "other" implies that according to the authors the algorithms of Grover and Shor are valid solutions to the problems to which they refer: an unacceptable statement for anyone who has full knowledge of the structure of the two algorithms, but also an excellent evidence of the strength of delusion in a context like this. The confusion at the root of everything lies in the attitude that is reached after investing time and energy in a question such as, for example, the rigorous demonstration of the properties of numbers that make Shor's algorithm work. One then thinks: the hard work that has been done is a success from a strictly mathematical point of view. Then one generalizes: it's a whole success. The effort necessary to master such a complex subject is enough to make us lose sight of all other considerations, and consequently it happens that the total failure of the attempt to find some useful quantum algorithm, despite being under the eyes of everyone, is lost under the blanket of mist that arises mainly from the fact of not clearly distinguishing software from hardware, and of continually mixing the logical characteristics of quantum algorithms with the physical characteristics of the hardware that should implement them, and with the a priori expectations concerning the hardware. Classical computer science, that is the one that has recorded immense successes for decades, is instead based on the rigorous distinction of the software layers from those of hardware.

This is a very severe comment, but unsatisfactory because it does not explain seriously how this situation came about: to clarify the context of Nielsen and Chuang's passage, a little history is needed. The basic idea, as we know, is to exploit the phenomena of entanglement and superposition to perform in parallel and ideally with a single machine cycle calculations that the Turing machine must perform in sequence and with repeated cycles. There are important scientific and technical problems that a computer based on the Turing machine cannot perform deterministically because it would be necessary to explore all the possible permutations of the elements involved, and the processing times would expand to last centuries, millennia or geological eras. To this class of problems belong logistics and optimization problems, such as the calculation of school timetables or the design of complex molecular structures. These problems are sometimes solved by not completely deterministic search techniques that introduce random elements, and sometimes, to date, they have no technical solution, in the sense that there is no efficient software to solve them. Sometimes there is the possibility of breaking down the problem into parts and entrusting the search for the solution of each part to separate processes, but some other times the problems to be faced are of such a nature that any modification of an element of the system to be analyzed can have consequences on the state of other elements located anywhere in the entire system, and therefore we cannot have the time savings allowed by parallel processing, because the search must take place in a single sequence managed by a single process: and in such case the solution is nowhere to be found due to the length of the processing process.

Now, the entanglement that is experienced in the subatomic phenomena of quantum experiments is a strong correlation between N qubits of a system which has the consequence that the measurement operation, while returning only one bit, gives information on the system as a whole. As for superposition, we know that it consists in the fact that by acting on qubits that represent a given initial state with binary information, certain probabilities are determined of detecting them in a different state after measurement, but for methodological reasons quantum physics considers probable states not still measured as if each had a potential reality that coexists alongside the potential realities of the others. Thus, from the fact that a qubit can be in a continuum of possible states expressed by complex amplitudes, comes the usual misleading expression, which is read in all newspaper articles, according to which a qubit can be simultaneously in both binary states 0 and 1, or have at the same time the spins ↑ and ↓, and other similar expressions, to whose repetition readers usually react with a sense of perplexed and astonished admiration.

From the two facts that entanglement is a natural correlation of multiple states, and that multiple probabilities can be seen as multiple coexisting realities, the idea was born of using it to perform calculations in parallel rather than in sequence. A nuclear physicist and a mathematician, Paul Benioff and Yuri Manin, first hinted at this idea in 1980, independently of each other, and in 1982 Richard Feynman[2] suggested a first generic model of a quantum computer. Feynman's idea was that it seems useless to break down quantum states in terms of binary representation to perform computations that require immense commitment of resources, and then reassemble them, and that therefore it was worth trying to use quantum phenomena as computers of themselves. If this were possible, then the calculator could be used for any order of phenomena that can be described with vectors and matrices of linear algebra. Feynman's expression is often quoted, and we repeat it here to observe that at first glance it sounds really plausible:

> "I'm not happy with all the analyses that go with just the classical theory, because nature isn't classical, dammit, and if you want to make a simulation of nature, you'd better make it quantum mechanical..."

At this point an attempt began to define in detail the theoretical machine corresponding to the quantum computer, and the works by David Deutsch (1985), Peter Shor (1994) and Lov Grover (1996) were published. The notation we have seen (still absent in Deutsch's first publication) was defined, and the question took the form we know; later many variations of the algorithms were made, which a website with an eloquent name[3] keeps carefully registered. From 2000 onwards there have been no news in terms of theory and mathematical models, while the construction of the hardware was attempted first with a few units of qubits, then with a few dozen. Bernhardt's book mentions the situation with a certain candour, speaking of Shor's algorithm[4]:

> The algorithm has been implemented, but just for small numbers. In 2001, it was used to factor 15 and in 2012 it factored 21.

Let us say that hackers, to whom Shor's algorithm will allow to prosper by breaking the encryption of our internet banking transactions, will need to live quite a long time to take this opportunity. In 2020 the construction seems to have given still very unstable results, and the implemented circuits seem usable only as hardware sources of sequences of random numbers. There is an

---

[2] Richard P. Feynman, "Simulating physics with computers", *International Journal of Theoretical Physics* volume 21, pp. 467–488 (1982).
[3] quantumalgorithmzoo.org.
[4] Bernhardt, p. 175.

experimental physicist, Mikhail Dyakonov, who has expressed a completely pessimistic view of the prospects of hardware[5].

The whole story could be described by distinguishing three periods. The period between 1985 and 1996 could be called that of the verification of the theoretical potential of the project, at the end of which no one wanted to acknowledge the failure and openly admit it. The second period, after 1996, is the sleepy and low-profile one: universities and computer industries kept the project alive because all in all having a quantum computing lab gives prestige and some advantage could always be obtained from it, but without the activity attracting public attention. The third period is that of the present bubble, with investments that continue to grow while no one cares to think about what a quantum computer could be used for once built. It should not be difficult to identify a decisive moment in the transition from the sleepy period to the bubble: an online article[6] on *Nature* shows that the acceleration can be observed from 2012 onwards, and it could be interesting to research the factor that triggered it.

Assuming that in the near future it will be possible to build systems with a certain number of qubits stable enough to give the expected results, no one in the world has the slightest idea of any profitable application which they could be used for, if not to execute some reversible gate and verify the five algorithms we know, devoid of any prospect of technical usage. Therefore, judging the situation with our feet on the ground, the story of the mathematical study of the potential of quantum computing carried out in the years from 1985 to 1996 appears to be an opportune and necessary but fruitless verification: the two basic concepts, entanglement that manifests itself in the impossibility of measuring the state of a qubit independently from the others, and superposition resulting from the consideration of probabilities as distinct potential realities, do not allow us to design a computer model of any kind. Quantum algorithms are pretended to be such when they are unable to give

---

[5] See the article "The Case Against Quantum Computing", 2018, in https://spectrum.ieee.org/computing/hardware/the-case-against-quantum-computing, and the book *Will We Ever Have a Quantum Computer?*, Springer 2020.

[6] "Quantum gold rush: the private funding pouring into quantum start-ups", 2 October 2019, https://www.nature.com/articles/d41586-019-02935-4

anything other than the superficially tautological repetition of the information implicit in the input.

However, there is a pattern of reasoning underlying the present fervour of initiatives and investments in the field of quantum computing, and the problem is that it is based on implicit premises that are usually taken for granted and withheld, or at most confusedly expressed. Let us try to clarify the premises, focusing on the words asserted with total seriousness in Nielsen and Chuang's book: "To design good quantum algorithms one must 'turn off' one's classical intuition for at least part of the design process, using truly quantum effects to achieve the desired algorithmic end", and let us rearrange what we know to understand their exact meaning, which corresponds to the mindset of who wrote them.

At the root of the whole story, there are numerous important problems for which a computer based on the Turing machine, analytical and sequential, is not suitable: either it is not able to find the solution in useful time, or calculation work is very heavy. The results of quantum mechanics led to make the two hypotheses that we know. The first hypothesis is that the natural correlation of the state of certain particles that occurs in isolated environments free of external disturbances, i.e. entanglement, can serve as a basis for performing parallel calculations. In a way this is a throwback to mechanical calculators, in which numerous gears rotate together and it is not necessary to decompose the data down to the minimum unit of information, the bit, to perform calculations. The difference is that in a mechanical calculator the correlation between the rotating elements must be designed by the manufacturer and is not ensured, because it depends on the proper functioning of the machine, while entanglement would offer a natural phenomenon in which certain elements align themselves spontaneously and necessarily: and this should be the advantageous factor of the quantum computational technique, not offered by any other natural phenomenon.

The second hypothesis is even stranger in the eyes of the ordinary mentality, and rests on certain "non-classical" methodological principles that belong to quantum mechanics, and of which there is no need to speak superficially here. The second hypothesis is that the continuum of real, or complex numbers, which represents the probabilities of a perturbed state of a qubit array before measurement, allows the manipulation of large amounts of data, ideally infinite, on the basis of a finite and limited set of input data. Let us take an example. A very complex optimization problem, and solved in a slow and never fully satisfactory way by the software available today, is that of school timetabling. When dealing with this problem, you have a weekly calendar that you have to fill with the teachers available, taking into account numerous rules of good formation: for example, a teacher who teaches a given subject for two hours a week wants this subject to be distributed in two different days, and so on. The fundamental problem in the search for solutions that respect the conditions of good formation is that each teacher teaches in several classes, and when he is in one he cannot be in another, because he cannot have the privilege of ubiquity: in the absence of this problem, finding the solution would be trivial. Now, if for example we have a week of 30 hours and a school of 20 classes, we have a total of $30 \times 20 = 600$ hours of lessons to fill, and the timetables that we could compose in all are 30^{600} (the formula is that of dispositions with repetition), of which a large number are physically impossible because they would require the gift of ubiquity from teachers, others are incorrect because they do not respect the rules of good formation, and some, or perhaps none, meet all the requirements. Of course, no computer can examine the 30^{600} possibilities in manageable times. With artificial intelligence techniques, we can find solutions by iterations of attempts that introduce random components and somehow emulate the research done by the human brain. But the hypothesis underlying the idea of quantum computation is different: we should start from a vector of the 600 elements whose ordered structure we are looking for, assign any values that do not satisfy what we are looking for, have a kind of vision of the necessary quantum gate, corresponding to the set of formal conditions to be satisfied, succeed in composing this gate through the universal elementary gates, and from this work we should derive the final ordered vector. The 30^{600} possible solutions should exist only in the continuum of complex amplitudes that describe the intermediate state of the system, and with them we should never have anything to do, because in the brain of the human being who manages the project (i.e., of the quantum software designer) there should be only input data and the composition of the quantum gates that correspond to the rule to find a solution. The situation should be identical to that of the "classical" programmer, who applying a rule does not have to develop the whole domain of cases to which it applies. Above, to introduce the Shor's algorithm, we have developed an elementary and yet efficient algorithm for finding the prime factors of eighteen-digit numbers: this does not mean we had to enumerate vectors of this size. If all this were to occur, the problems would disappear: vectors and matrices of dimensions impossible to manage would not be necessary, and it would not be necessary to explicitly calculate the U_f matrices, which would exist only in the composition of universal gates, as well as the prime factors of 64-bit numbers in a certain sense "exist" all together in the few lines of code that allows us to extract them.

So overall there are three hypotheses, not two. Two concern the mathematical aspect, and are those for which entanglement should allow calculations in parallel and the continuum of complex amplitudes should be used to perform calculations on vectors and matrices of otherwise unmanageable dimensions. The third hypothesis depends on the other two, but it does not concern either mathematics or quantum physics, but the nature of the animal species resulting from the evolution of the monkey to which we all have the honour of belonging: and it is that our cerebral apparatus should sooner or later adapt to the "non-classical" way of thinking and learn to see intuitively how to arrange the gates of an universal set in order to exploit the potential of the first two hypotheses, just as today's programmers know how to exploit the instructions of microprocessors, electronic designers know how to arrange the components in a circuit, masons know how to set up a brick wall, and so on: all things that chimpanzees could not do, and for which a creative and intuitive imagination is needed in addition to the analytical ability.

Now, what is disconcerting is that in order to understand that the entire building is based on these hypotheses, one must resort to one of the most complete texts on the subject, that of Nielsen and Chuang, which speaks of these things at the beginning of the first chapter[7], when the readers are not yet prepared to understand them and have not the slightest idea of what they will encounter in quantum algorithms; then the book does not deal with them any more again in the next 700 pages. Reading this section in full, we learn that the use of quantum circuits as a universal computer is no certainty at all, but nothing more than a conjecture formulated by Deutsch, about which the authors do not know what to think. On page 6 we read:

> At the time of writing it is not clear whether Deutsch's notion of a Universal Quantum Computer is sufficient to efficiently simulate an

---

[7] Section 1.1 from p. 1 to p. 12.

arbitrary physical system. Proving or refuting this conjecture is one of the great open problems...

but while reading this difficult book one is allowed to know that the theoretical possibility of a quantum computer is today a mere hypothesis, as well as the object of a rather generic definition, reading any other simpler source of learning this notion disappears completely, and the capacity of quantum computing is presented as a certainty, repeated all the more emphatically the more superficial the source of information is, to reach the maximum in web or newspaper articles, which never deal with anything other than the construction of the hardware.

The quantum algorithms that were studied thirty years ago reveal nothing favourable to the hypotheses: they break down analytically the data of their problems, and using inappropriate means arrive at very disappointing solutions even for those who approached them with cautious and limited expectations. The ability to compute in parallel is that which can be obtained by any hardware built ad hoc for a given function, the ability of the superposition to solve large numbers within itself is still entirely conjectural, no trace of it has been seen anywhere, and the ability of the human mind to compose quantum algorithms without making the explicit calculations is just as hypothetical. But despite this, everything written in these days of great enthusiasm for quantum computing seems to reveal that specialists strongly believe in the prospect of seeing the three hypotheses realized, and with such unanimity as to drag the not competent, but well informed public, to believe it with the same force and without the slightest doubt: for example, as I am writing these lines, I see that the issue of *The Economist* coming out just now[8] will have an article entitled "Wall Street's latest shiny new thing: quantum computing – A fundamentally new kind of computing will shake up finance – the question is when", which reflects well how everything is thought is focused on the issue of hardware building.

Both the reading public and the journalists who inquire about the question by interviewing specialists have no idea that the fundamental issue is not this, and that if the devil built a functioning quantum computer for us, nowadays no one would have any idea about its use. Specialists have a clear vision only when they have an overall vision of the problem, and probably the extreme division of

---

[8] December 19, 2020.

labour and skills keeps many insiders in a state of innocence. In particular, it is easy to imagine that those who have the mission of trying to make quantum phenomena work in a controlled and as stable way as possible in order to solve the hardware problem, must cope with problems of such difficulty as to allow them not to think at all of the software aspect, just as in classical computer science electronic technicians would never have been the right people to design operating systems, programming languages and more complex applications. As for those who know that the idea of using quantum phenomena and linear algebra as the principle of a universal computer is nowadays a mere conjecture, so much value they give to quantum mechanics achievements that they probably lightly commit the sin of omission not to emphasize this fact. After all, no one takes the trouble to ask them: "what could a quantum algorithm be used for, in detail?", and everyone is satisfied with the generic idea that it could be used to solve problems of higher complexity. In the attitude of the specialists there is an exact image of the mentality of the human environment in which this project grew up. Quantum computing is not the product of the vision of a genius, a precursor who has a confused vision at first, and on which he or she invests her energies for a long time, and for which the world is unprepared. On the contrary, this project is the collective product of a vast academic community that shares total confidence in a certain theory, that of quantum mechanics, and the undisputed consensus on this theory ends up lowering rather than raising the intellectual level of the community with respect to individuals who make it up. Any people who succeed in mastering the difficult concepts of quantum mechanics, live an experience so vivifying and exhilarating, and derive from it such occasions of social satisfaction, that then vulgar objections, such as the one that to make a quantum algorithm work it would be necessary to manage vectors of the size of millions of figures and in thirty years no one has imagined a remedy, seem completely irrelevant to them. Or rather, they get used to not even listening to these objections in their heart, which nevertheless appear to anyone having a thorough knowledge of the matter, because when the social game of a community revolves all around enthusiastic announcements and optimism at all costs, doubt becomes an anti-social practice with a price too high to pay. And so, for the unprejudiced, the situation becomes that described by the tale of the emperor's suit, which ends when some innocent people naively assert that the king is naked.

7.4 Conclusion for investors

According to the author this book, the quantum computer project is an illusion resulting from the interaction of many different factors: the enormous prestige of quantum physics, and above all of the so-called Copenhagen interpretation; the difficulty in training people who have an overview of the whole problem; the cultural phenomenon born around the time of First World War, an attitude alive and well in our present, whereby all people who have a certain level of education tend to grant a complete credit full of admiration to the ideas of non-classical physics, even when they do not have any knowledge and understanding of it. The author of this book would not bet a penny on the success of the project, for the opinion that has grown in his mind about the general approach to the whole question. When the first computers such as Mark I and ENIAC were built after 1940, it is true that shortly before had been formulated Turing's theoretical hypotheses on the universal ability of a machine with given characteristics to solve algorithms, but the projects were also based on the clear knowledge of the simplest profitable use that could be made of them. That is, no one had any idea of the operating systems and architectures to come, but how those computers could be used to produce tables of numerical values of useful functions was well known before the machine was built. Now, on the opposite, the context is profoundly different: the quantum computer project does not arise from a precise vision of the concrete, however simple, case to which it could be applied, but from the unlimited trust that is placed in some general statements of a philosophical and methodological rather than physical nature, and which should follow and not precede a technological project; and an attempt is made to derive the project from these general propositions that have become prejudices so strong as to make people blind to the evident failure of verification, to the point that the specialists, while aware of the situation, describe Grover's and Shor's algorithms as if they were successes, when they instead witness the opposite, i.e. that no one has ever conceived how entanglement and superposition could seriously be used to obtain non-trivial computational results.

So the author of this book would bet on failure, but this, mind you, is an opinion that as such does not matter. This book was written to allow investors to decide whether to invest financial resources in projects related to the quantum computing, and the conclusions therefore consist of some questions that investors, in their interest, would do well to ask themselves, and above all in the exact identification of the object of the investment risk.

Those who invest in projects associated with the construction of quantum computers, either investors of own capitals or investment fund managers, are now in the hands of experts, and are forced to decide on the basis of experts advice. Now, from the point of view of a person starting from scratch and wanting to get informed, there are several possible scenarios. If we go back to the beginning, and forget what we have learned about algorithms, we must recognize that once a quantum computer is built it could fall into one of these cases, and be:

1. fully unnecessary.

2. useful for something, for specific problems.

3. very useful, next to traditional computers.

4. useful to the point of superseding traditional computers.

In cases 2, 3 and 4, the evaluation of an investment should be based on a detailed analysis of the costs and benefits and would need the opinion of the quantum physicist who knows the problems of hardware construction to answer the question: what is the probability of succeeding in building an efficient quantum computer, with what time and cost? And therefore, in cases 2, 3 and 4, a book like ours would only give a partial answer, indicating what could be the use and benefits of a functioning quantum computer, but giving no information about the time and cost.

If, on the other hand, the study of algorithms led us to the conclusion of case 1, the knowledge of the purely Information Technology aspect would be sufficient to decide not to invest: if a machine is designed in such a way that once built it would be useless, every penny invested in the enterprise is destined to be lost. If someone brought us a project for a car with square wheels, we would not need to build it to know that we would not go very far away. It is true that the research could bear unexpected collateral fruits, and that many discoveries and inventions have arisen from research with different aims. But in this specific story, the research has its roots in a context of misunderstandings and muddled and confused thinking: investing in quantum computing means trusting a way of thinking that instead of facing the failure of the attempt to use quantum phenomena for computing, has found a refuge in dogma, and asserts that a failure is a success for no other reason than suggestion and prejudice. And to tell something of the confusional state of the question, there is still an important observation to be made: while, as we have seen, the most rigorous treaties are led by the very fact of treating the subject with completeness to recognize that no technique for using a possibly functioning quantum computer has ever been conceived, the rest of what is written avoids the subject of software as a taboo. There are a large number of web pages reporting on investment and research developments, but what is invariably talked about is the construction of hardware and the effort to get qubits stable enough to function in a controlled manner. Sometimes an announcement is made that this or that experiment has reached a new level of "quantum supremacy", but when reading carefully it always turns out that a certain device has worked according to its design and the output has been sampled; then the output is compared to the result of a calculation, but it is always a calculation of values of the function that describes that specific hardware configuration, without the hardware being able to calculate anything different. And this is very similar to arguing (but no one would make a fool of him or herself with such a claim) that a blade of grass grown to a height of 10 centimetres has calculated the function of its own growth by solving a very complicated system of equations: which can be said as a joke, but does not transform a blade of grass in a computer, just as everything else that works according to rules described by functions is not therefore a calculator of these functions. But in short, the main fact is that software is not talked about, and it is likely that the community working around the quantum computing project is censored in a spontaneous and completely automatic process: everyone avoids talking about what they don't know, everyone thinks that others have better knowledge of things about which the accounts do not add up, and the community as a whole has an interest in making the subject go unnoticed.

What do investors want to do now? Do they want to make the act of faith suggested by Nielsen and Chuang, and believe not only that the conjecture that a quantum computer can exist is well founded, but also that a mutation of the human mind will soon take place, so that we shall be able to design efficient algorithms for a machine which, as far as we know today, is useless? Let them invest, if they believe, but they should understand that they are not betting on the success of building a functioning quantum computer corresponding to today's theoretical model, which could happen in the next few years, but on the possibility that men will receive the gift of an evolution of their faculties in the way desired by quantum physicists, rather than according to Darwin's natural selection, and so then they will imagine what to do with it. It is not to seem witty that I say these words, but to try to express the surrealistic situation of this story: huge investments are being made on a conjecture whose verification in thirty years has not given any fruit, and investors know that they are betting on the possibility of building a certain hardware that has its prototype in some experiments, but they are completely clueless about the fact that they are also investing in a (very fragile) conjecture regarding the necessary software. The author's opinion is that therefore the project is doomed to failure: the investors will draw the conclusion that seems plausible to them.

If they share the pessimistic conclusion, savvy investors will consider that the current fervour of investment in quantum computing projects is a bubble, similar to the many bubbles that have exploded in the world since the time of speculation about Dutch tulips, around 1637. There is, however, one difference with the bubbles experienced in history, which makes the story of quantum computing singular and unique. Bubbles are generally based on the prospect of unlimited rise: many realize that a given asset or financial instrument is reaching prices that are unrelated to the use value or the factors necessary to produce the asset, and yet they buy it, with the confidence of being able to sell before the rise stops and prices collapse. Whoever succeeds in doing this, appropriates the capital lost by those who do not succeed, and those who do not succeed fail, either because they made bad forecasts or because they were so naive as to believe in the miracle of unlimited rise of prices. The present quantum computer bubble, on the other hand, is not based on the prospect of unlimited rise, but on public confidence in this reasoning: since quantum mechanics is a very high intellectual achievement, then its technological application must necessarily be very efficient as well. The non-competent public believes it in all good faith, to the point of exempting the experts from explaining how a quantum computer should work to perform calculations up to expectations. The experts, whose role should be to illustrate the arbitrariness of this deduction, instead are the first to take it as valid, they too in good faith, perhaps fearing unconsciously that the failure of the technological project would cast a shadow even on the theoretical part and would undermine its present supremacy.

7. Perspectives of quantum computing

Appendix: use of the QcNooq project

The *QcNooq* project is available for download at the page: www.zonabit.it/QcNooq. Are available separately:

- the setup of the *QcNooq* executable program for Microsoft Windows (QcNooqSetup.exe);

- the source code (QcNooq.zip).

If you don't want to compile *QcNooq*, simply install the software and run it to check the output of the emulation code as you read the book.

If you want to compile *QcNooq* under Windows, unzip QcNooq.zip in any folder and open the project. The source code includes a project for Microsoft Visual Studio (QcNooq.vcproj) in a version from a few years ago. Any recent version of Microsoft Visual Studio will convert the project automatically. The project has 32-bit configuration for compatibility with older versions, but users can easily compile for 64-bit, and will experience some slight increase in execution speed

There is also another project (QcNooqConsole.vcproj) that allows you to compile *QcNooq* as a console application, without a Windows GUI: this does not give any advantage in a Windows environment, but can help the porting of *QcNooq* as a console application in a different environment.

If you want to compile *QcNooq* in an environment other than Windows, you must use the code following the instructions below.

1. some modules should not be included in the project because they contain the implementation of the Windows interface, and are the following:

```
QcNooqButton.h
QcNooqDialog.h
QcNooqDlg.h
QcNooqStatic.h
QcNooq_ReadMe.h
stdafx.cpp
QcNooqButton.cpp
QcNooqDialog.cpp
QcNooqDlg.cpp
QcNooqStatic.cpp
QcNooq_ReadMe.cpp
```

2. some modules make up a fully portable library of mathematical functions, and can be recompiled without difficulty in any environment:

```
QCM_math.h
QCM_tools.h
QCM_complex0.cpp
QCM_format0.cpp
QCM_matrix0.cpp
QCM_matrix1.cpp
QCM_procs0.cpp
QCM_state0.cpp
QCM_tools0.cpp
QCM_vector0.cpp
```

3. the last group of sources corresponds to the chapters of the book:

```
3:   QCP_matrix.cpp
4:   QCP_bitqubit.cpp
5:   QCP_gates.cpp
6.1:  QCP_deutsch.cpp
6.2:  QCP_deutsch_josza.cpp
6.3:  QCP_simon.cpp
6.4:  QCP_grover.cpp
6.5:  QCP_shor.cpp
```

and for the console application there is an entry point sample in:

```
QCNooqConsole.cpp
```

The source code of the modules of the third group contains first the implementation of the dialog that hosts buttons and other objects in the Windows interface, and then the code corresponding to the examples discussed in the corresponding chapters. Throughout the program, the application code concerning the Windows interface is under the condition of the definition of the symbol QCNOOQ_WINDOWS, which must not be defined outside the Windows environment, nor in the console version. In most cases the code under the QCNOOQ_WINDOWS condition can be simply omitted, and only in some cases is it necessary to intervene to provide a requested data input. For example, to test Shor's algorithm we find the case in which the number N is read from a box in the Windows environment, and must be fixed in the sources or asked to the user:

```
#ifdef QCNOOQ_WINDOWS
  m_edit_number_16.GetWindowText(buf, 200);
   only_digits(buf);
#else
  strcpy(buf, "15"); // to be done: input number
```

```
#endif
```

In all cases, the code uses the following function for output, implemented with three variants:

```
extern void ListMatrix(char init, char *comment,
 int mrow, int ncol, qx *mtr, int hexacomment );
extern void ListMatrix(char init, char *comment,
 int mrow, int ncol, qx *mtr );
extern void ListMatrix(char init, char *comment);
```

which directs the output to the two boxes provided by the Windows interface, the upper one for generic information and the lower one to represent the matrices resulting from the calculations. The code of ListMatrix() is located in the QCM_tools0.cpp file and must be implemented in the new environment, redirecting the output to the console or to the available graphic interface. The function to be modified is global_ListMatrix(), of which in QCM_tools0.cpp there are both the Windows version and a rudimentary version for a console application.

The program built outside the Windows environment must have an entry point that must include the definitions of the modules with the QCP_ prefix that you want to test, allocate the appropriate class and call the function to be tested. For example, to try the first of the tests provided while reading the book, multiplication of a vector by a matrix, the program will be:

```
#include <stdio.h>
// include and create the QCP_ modules and
// CQCP_ classes you want to test:
#include "QCP_matrix.h"
static CQCP_matrix test_matrix;
int main (int argc, char *argv[] )
{
char buf[100];
 // call the test you want to perform
 test_matrix.QCF_Mul_Vector_Matrix();
 printf ("TEST FINISHED - PRESS ENTER"); gets(buf);
}
```

and for any other case, all you have to do is include the appropriate QCP_xxx.h module, allocate the class and call the test. The code inside the classes with the prefix CQCP_ can be modified as desired to study the behaviour of the algorithms in different conditions.

Appendix: use of the QcNooq project

Back cover

This book is aimed at people who simply know the basics of computer programming. It does not require any notion of physics and allows its readers to understand with total accuracy and in the simplest way the use that could be made of a quantum computer, by explaining step by step how to write a software to emulate its operation. The usual expression that a qubit "is an object that can be simultaneously in both binary states 0 and 1" will lose all the aura of mystery that surrounds it, and readers will understand exactly its meaning and implications for computing without the need for any knowledge of physics. The book describes quantum computing by considering it strictly from a computer science point of view, simply as a machine that is capable of transforming a given input into a given output using any suitable physical principle to work, and thus allows to become completely familiar with quantum gates and with the most famous quantum algorithms. The only condition is that the readers are familiar with some programming language and with the basic concepts of classical computer science: those who have this knowledge will easily follow the description of quantum algorithms and understand the software emulation that is implemented in the book, and will also have fun running and testing it with their own PC.

The knowledge acquired through this book is of vital importance to *investors* because it allows them to judge independently on the risk of investing in this technology. It has been written for *programmers* because the knowledge of basics of computer science is useful to understand exactly what a quantum computer, once built, could be used for. But this understanding is also essential for *investors* who must evaluate whether and how much it is appropriate to risk investing in the development of quantum computing. Therefore, even *investors* (private investors, consultants, managers of financing funds for technological enterprises, etc.) who want to decide on the allocation of resources in quantum computing with full knowledge of the stakes, must know this book, and if they do not personally own the necessary prerequisites, they can use it by hiring some trusted computer expert to read it, understand it and report on the result.

Alberto Palazzi

A scholar of history and philosophy of science, and designer of computer algorithms for the solution of higher complexity problems, the author of this book is a member of the *QcNooq* consulting team (www.zonabit.it/qcnooq), whose mission is to provide investors the clarity of view necessary to decide on investments in quantum computing.